WOMEN WHO
SOAR

STORIES OF **CHALLENGING** THE

STATUS QUO AND **BREAKING**

THE GLOBAL PATRIARCHY

LABELLE NAMBANGI

Minneapolis

ISBN 13: 978-1-63489-120-2
eISBN: 978-1-63489-131-8

Library of Congress Catalog Number: 2018935097
Printed in the United States of America
First Printing: 2018

22 21 20 19 18   5 4 3 2 1

Cover design by Nupoor Gordon
Interior design by Kim Morehead

Wise Ink Creative Publishing
837 Glenwood Ave.
Minneapolis, MN 55405
www.wiseinkpub.com

DEDICATION

This book is dedicated to my babies: Lisa, Jasmine, Jereon, Kyron, Ginger-Bella, Joy, Inez, Jireh, and Sean. May you grow up to be women and men of change.

And to my beloved maternal grandmother, Elizabeth Baliki Nambangi "Mom": You are an epitome of a woman of change and I have watched you in awe as you live your life with such grace, class and dignity. Thank you for being a living expression of sisterhood, kindness, resourcefulness, self-restraint, resilience and most of all for loving me deeply. I aspire to be an empowered woman with vision and grace just like you. I am honored to be your first grandchild.

TABLE OF

CONTENTS

FOREWORD

I met LaBelle Nambangi in 1996 when we were both students at Saker Baptist High School, an all-girls boarding school in Limbe, Cameroon. Even then, her gift was apparent—she had a unique capacity for uplifting those of us around her to be our best. Her words were positive, her actions exemplary. She loved and encouraged the idea of a sisterhood. In an environment where girls often found themselves competing against each other, LaBelle believed in and promoted the notion of women being each other's allies, recognizing that through our support of each other we could learn, grow, and become our very best selves. By the time she was a tenth-grader, she had adopted younger students, taking them under her wings as her little sisters. She watched out for them even though she was still a teenager.

I cannot think of a person more equipped to write this honest and timely story about women challenging the status quo than LaBelle. She has spent over ten years preparing young immigrant girls for college, building their self-esteem and confidence, and enabling them to develop a can-do spirit. She has dedicated herself to helping low-income women improve their careers and develop financial literacy skills in order to become self-sufficient and freely design the lives they want for themselves and their families. She reminds women that they are capable of great things and are complete by themselves.

To combat patriarchal norms and help build a world where every human is treated with equal dignity and respect, LaBelle has written a book of wisdom replete with practical steps on how to challenge the roadblocks women face. She calls on women to become allies to one another as opposed to the old paradigm of rivals and competitors. She calls on men to become champions and supporters of women's fight for equality, because we all suffer when women are held back from being their authentic selves.

In this insightful book, LaBelle shares stories of women who refused to accept the stories they'd been told about themselves and the world around them. She writes of daring women who decided to author their own stories, awakened to the truth that only they should decide how to live their lives. These women changed not only their lives but also the lives of other women of their generation and the generation after them.

LaBelle gives moving testimony from her visits with the teen mothers at the Teen Mother's Academy Institute in Buea, Cameroon, whose only wish is to get an education and become self-reliant. She writes about determined women like Dr. Verna Price, whose mission is to empower and equip young girls who are tomorrow's leaders to succeed in school and life. She shares the story of Joy McBrien, who turned her personal pain into advocating for victims of rape and sexual assaults by providing them with employment opportunities.

She shares the experiences of women like Marcia Malzahn, who immigrated to the US from Nicaragua, against all odds broke the glass ceiling in a predominately male industry, and now provides educational opportunities for other women to do same in their lives; and Hilda Bih, a disabled woman who attained her education in a country with no provision for the disabled, becoming an advocate for those with disabilities and a champion for girl's education. In the stories of these women, we see the virtues of courage and wisdom and an abiding passion to make the world better.

LaBelle makes a powerful argument for why men must join the fight for women's rights. She shares the story of her maternal grandfather, who, unlike many in his generation, fervently supported his daughter's educational ambitions. His relentless belief in women's empowerment ultimately compelled other men in his village to recognize the necessity of educating girls and providing equal opportunities for both genders. She shares the story of three men who proudly identify with the pro-feminist movement, an identification that can bring about no small change in the world if words are coupled with positive action.

Considering our current sociopolitical climate, where sexism reigns and women are punished for having been born women, this book could not be more needed. It is a book that should be read by anyone who desires to awaken to the truth that we must all play a role in putting an end to prevalent injustice.

A great teacher once wrote that women will lead us to the day when we all live in a better world. I believe so too, and I am thankful for women like LaBelle, who are at the forefront of this evolution.

I hope you will enjoy reading about these brave women and men and will apply whatever lessons you learn from them to your life. My wish for you is that, through the stories of the struggles and triumphs and awakenings of these extraordinary women who challenged what they had been taught to believe so that they could free themselves, you will discover your own essence.

I hope you'll join LaBelle on this journey of awakening, and I hope you'll discover the truth about your own greatness— and by so doing cause darkness to disappear with the light that shines within you. It is my fervent wish that you will read this book carefully and allow it to offer your guidance.

—Imbolo Mbue

INTRODUCTION

*The empowered woman is powerful beyond
measure and beautiful beyond description.*
—Steve Maraboli

August 4, 2000, was the day I arrived in Minnesota with my brothers Cyril and Sidney, extremely exhausted after the tedious twenty-hour flight from Douala, Cameroon. Our first stop was Charles de Gaulle Airport in Paris, followed by O'Hare International Airport in Chicago before finally arriving at Minneapolis–St. Paul International Airport. We were reuniting with our mother, who immigrated to the United States in 1992 after receiving a prestigious Hubert H. Humphrey Fellowship to study journalism at the University of Minnesota. I was excited to see her but also apprehensive about new beginnings—I was still finding myself and not sure of my true calling.

After two months in Minnesota, I got my first job in retail and quickly realized that it wasn't the field I belonged in. I excelled at my job and became the go-to person but didn't get much satisfaction from the monotony of it. I enrolled in school to study accounting but also realized I wasn't passionate about that field either; I continued on with the degree, uncertain of how to navigate the system.

Meanwhile, my mother was working as a domestic violence advocate at a women's shelter where she met a few African clients. She saw that these women needed more—there were language and cultural barriers between them and their advocates, who often encouraged the women to find menial labor jobs rather than to truly live up to their potentials. It was easier to send them to minimum wage jobs than to understand their interests, talents, and aspirations. My mother's new calling became rectifying this problem. She soon learned that there were many more African women in the Twin Cities in need of the same services as the women at the shelter.

In 2002, she started a nonprofit called the Minnesota African Women's Association (MAWA) for African immigrant and refugee women in the Twin Cities. The organization was created to help African women who were still being held back by cultural practices deeply rooted in patriarchy. MAWA's mission is to advocate for African women and their families, promote education, provide tools for financial independence, and provide health education. In essence, it strives to enable African immigrant women to become *women of change*. A woman of change believes that women are inherently equal to men and that we all will benefit once societies and cultures reflect this natural equality. She advocates for herself and her sisters in both large and small ways, through work, family, and politics.

I was surprised to receive many calls from non-African women wondering how they, too, could benefit from MAWA's programs. I learned that women from all cultures, including those born in the United States, need support to become women of change, though some need additional help due to educational gaps, cultural constructs, and religious beliefs.

After my mother worked with the MAWA women for two years, they asked her to create a program for their daughters. These girls were new to the country and faced isolation and discrimination at school, which led to low self-esteem and little sense of worth. My mother created the African Girls' Initiative for Leadership and Empowerment (AGILE) program in 2004 to combat the low rate of high school graduation and college enrollment combined with a high rate of teenage pregnancy in African girls, predominantly within war-torn communities.

As an immigrant from Cameroon, I witnessed and experienced the patriarchal culture—both in Africa and the United States—that so often holds these young women back from their potential. I volunteered with AGILE from the start and greatly enjoy working with the girls. AGILE's main mission is to help better prepare young African girls in the Twin Cities for college, build their self-esteem and leadership skills, teach financial literacy, provide health education (to avoid teenage pregnancy and sexually transmitted infections), and encourage the girls to become advocates for themselves and other girls. I've worked with over three thousand girls over thirteen years and it has been an amazing and fulfilling experience. I took this as my life's mission and calling—to empower girls and women beyond the ones I work with.

In honor of International Women's Day 2016, I asked the AGILE girls to talk about their role models and why they looked up to those women. It's my tradition to give the girls assignments that build their public speaking skills and self-confidence, as well as to teach them about influential women around the world. As is to be expected with teenagers, most of them listed celebrities and other famous women as role models. I couldn't help but notice the absence of influential women in their own lives. "Why don't you include your own mothers and the women in your community as role models?" I asked. I wasn't prepared for their responses:

"My mother does nothing but cook and clean, and doesn't work outside the house."

"My mother hands her paycheck over to my father every week and is never allowed to spend money for herself."

"My mother stays with my abusive father."

"The women in my community don't support each other—they act jealously and blame each other for their problems."

"The women in my community are treated like children by their husbands. They don't stand up to the men in their lives."

Their words were cold, agonizing, disheartening, and, in certain cases, bitter. Surely, if these girls didn't see role models in the women around them, they must see something special in the celebrities that they pinpointed. I asked, "What do you see in the role models you identified?"

"They're powerful."

"They're independent."

"They have their own money."

"They make their own decisions."

"They're surrounded by beautiful things that they achieved for themselves."

"They're beautiful."

"They're happy."

When I asked if they thought that they could be as successful and influential as these women, most of the girls responded negatively, stating that the women they admired were different:

"They were raised in affluence. Their parents could afford to send them to fancy schools or special classes."

"They're a different race, ethnicity, religion, and culture. They're not bound by the same cultural and religious expectations as we are."

"Society favors their race, class, and ethnicity."

Why weren't these girls seeing role models in their own communities? Why did they identify with these celebrity women instead of their own mothers? It seemed that there were so few encouraging examples of independent women in their lives that this lack of role models limited their self-worth. They considered their mothers to be weak, yet their visions for independence and success were grandiose and un-realistic by most standards. They didn't have models of inde-pendence in their own lives and therefore didn't believe that they could achieve these desired living standards.

I was alarmed and saddened by their responses. I'm lucky because I've always looked up to the women in my family—my grandmother, "Mom"; my mother, Melissa; and my aunts Beatrice, ("Auntie Dawdaw"), Inez ("Ma E."), and Auntie San-dra.They're all women's advocates and excellent role models of independence. My experience was standard for a mid-dle-class girl in Cameroon: I was raised knowing that an edu-cation would open doors and give me independence, and that a man would only treat me poorly if I let him. These beliefs have nothing to do with race. Many girls from poorer fami-lies in Cameroon and around Africa had different pressures: they were discouraged from pursuing higher education by their parents and community members to avoid intimidating potential husbands. Many girls were told that the best they could hope for was to get married and have a man take care of them. This is not unusual. From a very young age, girls are constantly told that they're valued for their ability to cook and clean rather than their intellect, passions, or talents. MAWA and AGILE exist because these damaging ideologies follow the girls when they immigrate to Western countries.

Half of the girls in the program are first-generation Americans and the other half immigrated into the United

States from various African countries. I was curious if non-African girls would have the same response on the topic of role models. I asked the girls to invite their friends from other races and ethnicities—Asians, Caucasians, Indians, African-Americans, and Latinas—to participate in some of the discussions. One thing was certain: most of the girls admired someone whom they didn't know—a celebrity or an influential woman from television. Most of these girls agreed that they had little to nothing in common with their role models. These non-Africans girls also didn't consider most of the women in their lives powerful. This showed me that all girls, regardless of race, ethnicity, religion, and culture, need positive female role models in their lives.

We discussed the ways that women are held back globally and the common issues that they face. The girls listed the following issues:

- There is a pay gap between women and men
- There are fewer women in government and leadership
- Religious systems are rooted in patriarchy
- Women have limited access to education and resources
- Women are encouraged to be in competition with each other in stories, movies, and life

The girls agreed that these issues are faced by women and girls all over the world (but are more evident in certain cultures), and we agreed that we still live in patriarchal societies. It dawned on me after this exercise that women find it difficult to draw inspiration from other women, especially those around us, because we're used to our gender being presented as weak, inferior, and subordinate, and we're accustomed to laws that encourage gender discrimination. Perhaps this is because we're raised to view men as the leaders, starting with our fathers. We aren't encouraged to see ourselves as whole and complete in our own rights. Women are often portrayed in movies as happy and fulfilled only when they have men in their lives. When we are taught about women who faced adversity, they are usually from the past, live far away from us, or are famous. We present these ladies as special, as though ordinary women can't achieve what they have. Society usually presents wealthy, famous women as powerful and important, teaching young girls that only privileged, celebrity women can be influential. Even independence, happiness, and fulfillment are tied to class and privilege.

The AGILE girls didn't consider the women in their families and communities as strong and independent given their class, culture, and ethnicity. They saw celebrities and other influential women as their role models because these women were financially independent, in control of their own lives, and resilient. They were problem solvers who stood up to men and went after their dreams. This celebrity worship conditions young girls to believe that the women in their families and communities aren't as bold and courageous as famous women, which makes it difficult for girls to find inspiration and success within themselves and in their environment. I truly believe that when we assume we can only find inspiration from people far away, success eludes us.

In light of this scary revelation, I realized that young girls need to learn how to become women of change immediately. They need to become their own role models and role models for the generations that follow. It was something that I learned from my grandmother, mother, and aunties, but that many girls don't have the benefit of seeing in their cultures or environments, let alone their households.

From my work, I learned that we can become women of change by challenging the status quo. This means that we can take a variety of actions:

- Recognize the assumptions and prejudices at play within you. See the damaging internalized beliefs that you hold for yourself and others. What beliefs do you have about yourself or other women that have held you back?
- Notice things around and within you. What examples of oppression and prejudice toward women do you see in your own life and in the lives of those around you?
- Recognize your role as a woman of change for the next generation. We can all be women of change within our careers and places in society. You don't have to dedicate your life to activism to make a difference. How can you make choices to support women within your current role?
- Encourage other men and women to become people of change—beacons in the global resistance happening to resist patriarchal dynamics.

My hope is that this book empowers and inspires you through the stories of people of change. Join them in challenging whatever status quo is holding you back from becoming your authentic self, and do the same for others. Recognize your value and realize that you are a complete being so that you can become a person of change, identify your role for the next generation, and make a positive impact in others' lives. Each chapter contains stories of independent women who recognize that they are equal to men. They see the needs of other women and are actively empowering themselves and their sisters. There are also men of change who recognize that men and women are inherently equal. They are taking an active role in educating other men on the importance of equality and how much stronger the world would be if both genders were given equal opportunities and could work together.

When I realized that I was a woman of change, it dawned on me that I have an added responsibility to lead by example at all times. I was challenged to rid myself of any form of comparison and competition toward my fellow women; to see the light and goodness in every woman I encounter. Due to this awakening, when I see another woman these days . . .

I see myself.

I see a friend.

I see a sister.

I see a mother.

I see an ally.

I see the first teacher to every child.

I see strength.

I see the backbone to every economy.

I see a person trying to break a glass ceiling like I am.

What do you see when you see another woman? How can you become her advocate?

TEACHING WOMEN

According to the United Nations (UN),[1] the gender wage gap will not close for seventy years at its current rate. The International Labour Organization says that the difference in earnings between men and women has barely changed in twenty years. Women across the world earn 77 percent of the amount paid to men, a figure that has improved by only three percentage points in the past twenty years. According to Bank of America Merrill Lynch's latest "Transforming World Atlas" report on gender income disparity around the world, between 2011 and 2014, a woman earned $76 for every $100 that a man was paid. Even in New Zealand, the country with the smallest pay gap, women still earned 5 percent less than men.[2] In addition to the gender wage gap, there exists a similar gap among women of different races, making African-American women fall further and further behind due to the lack of strategy, vision, and advocacy around these disparities. The latest data from the US Census

---

1   Alexandra Topping, "Gender pay gap will not close for 70 years at current rate, says UN," *Guardian*, March 5, 2015.

2   Akin Oyedele, "There's no country where women make more than men," *Business Insider*, March 23, 2016.

Bureau show minuscule changes to the wage gap, especially for women of color. Race and ethnicity have always created a dividing line in the United States, and this extends deep into the area of employment. The pay gap affects all women, but it doesn't affect all women equally.[3] An article on Black Enterprise gives detailed statistics on the disparity in wage between the same gender among difference races.[4]

3   "How does Race Affect the Gender Wage Gap?" American Association of Universtiy Women. https://www.aawu.org/2014/04/03/race-and-the-gender-wage-gap

4   "Report Sheds Grim Details on Black Women's Net Worth." Black Enterprise.   https://www.blackenterprise.com/the-net-worth-of-the-single-black-woman-devil-in-the-details/

CHAPTER ONE

FINANCIAL INDEPENDENCE

I have only one request.
I do not ask for money
Although I have need of it,
I do not ask for meat . . .
I have only one request,
And all I ask is
That you remove
The roadblock
From my path.
—Okot p'Bitek, *Song of Lawino*

On January 12, 2016, the phone rang repeatedly for about a minute before I could get myself out of bed to pick it up. That early morning phone call came from my Auntie Dawdaw in Cameroon.

"Yes, baby, it's me. Sorry for waking you up."

"It's okay, Auntie Dawdaw. Everything okay?"

"No. Mami Alice just passed away this morning and Mom is very sad about her death. You know she's been sick for so long. Please tell the others. You all need to send in contributions for the funeral quickly, as we intend to have it done in two weeks. I'm on my way to the village this very moment."

"Weh, poor Mom, her only living aunt is gone. Tell her and Mami Alice's children *ashia*. Tell them we send our condolences. Weh, poor Mami Alice. May her gentle soul rest in peace."

Mami Alice was my maternal great-grandaunt and I knew her well when I was a child. She was courageous—not afraid to stand up to a bully. One of my favorite memories of Mami Alice was when she broke up a fight that some bullies had started with my Uncle Victor. Though she was much smaller than the men—only four feet eleven inches tall—she exuded power and strength that they did not, and they backed down.

She had a close relationship with her niece, my grandmother, "Mom." Mom was not only fond and protective of her aunt, she watched out for her best interests, as well. Mom managed Mami Alice's tiny assets for years, which eventually made her one of the few women in the village who had some financial stability.

I was raised by my grandparents (Mom and Dad) throughout primary school in the community of Bekondo. Holidays were spent either with my mother in the capital city of Yaoundé or with my Auntie Dawdaw in the town of Buea. During those years, I realized the challenges that women face not just in my community but in the entire country. The problems of financial abuse, financial infidelity, and financial illiteracy plagued most Cameroonian women, including those in Bekondo. Financial abuse is when your partner has complete control of finances and limits your access to bank accounts; in financial infidelity, you are kept ignorant about your finances by your partner; lastly, financial illiteracy is when you have no knowledge about how to control money. Financial abuse was so rampant and normalized in my community that most women didn't own property, not even the land they toiled on daily, even though these women were and remain the majority of the agricultural workforce. Despite the fact that every Cameroonian citizen has the legal right to land ownership, it doesn't actually happen; land rights are regulated by statutes, customs, and, at times, informal arrangements.

The constant reminder that the man is the head of the home and provider for the family favors men and gives them the authority to make all decisions as they see fit. In some communities and homes, women are expected to give their paychecks and earned wages to their husbands; those who don't are labeled stubborn and are sometimes thrown out of their homes. This is why most of the women in Bekondo came to Mom, who was financially independent, to ask for personal loans (with promises to pay her back). Mom was kind-hearted and gave out loans, often not receiving her money back. In some cases, the same women who had yet to repay previous loans would reapproach Mom, pleading and crying for help. Mom heard them out and either gave them a second loan or explored other methods for the women to earn money. Mom gave loans to a few women to start businesses, but they still couldn't repay their loans because they gave their earnings to their husbands, who mismanaged the funds.

Mami Alice was eternally grateful that she was able to live with less financial worry since Mom managed her assets. Mami Alice was aware of the financial hardships that the women in Bekondo were dealing with and the amount of money Mom lost from giving out loans. She approached Mom with a brilliant and progressive idea: they could combine forces and became pioneers in women's financial freedom. As women of change, they were the first in my village to recognize that African women had to help each other to gain independence and become financially self-sufficient. They saw that their struggles didn't have to be theirs alone—that no woman has to struggle alone, and that women were stronger together and had the power to overcome oppression.

MOM AND MAMI ALICE

When Mami Alice was in her sixties, she decided to create a women's association based on her community's needs. Dubbed the Oroko Women's Association of Bekondo (*Oroko* is a tribe in Cameroon, and Bekondo is a village within that tribe), it helped women save money together. Most of the women, including Mami Alice, couldn't read or write, so she approached Mom, who was educated, to take over running, organizing, and hosting the monthly meetings while Mami Alice focused on recruiting members. In the meetings, women ritually put aside their money; however, they could save much of it for later. Mom opened a bank account for the women to deposit into each month beginning in January, and they withdrew their money in December in time for the holidays and back-to-school preparation. A treasurer kept track of everybody's contributions. This gave the women a sense of security, and they grew in their financial independence over time. The women also organized a *njangi* or *susu*—a kind of savings group where each member contributes a set amount of money every month, and each month the total sum is given to one person. This is repeated monthly until each member has received the same total amount. It's an informal means of collecting and saving money that allows members who aren't disciplined with their money or wanted a large sum of money for an investment within a shorter time period to save the sum needed. Some members who could afford extra savings were part of the regular savings initiative and the *njangi*.

Mom also hosted and was president of the Christian

Women's Fellowship (CWF) group; she introduced the financial savings concept to the group and opened a bank account for them. Mom encouraged and taught the women in both the Oroko Women's Association and the CWF group about the importance of saving money and various ways to grow their savings.

To the women of the Oroko Women's Association and the CWF group, financial stability meant the freedom to make financial decisions that impacted their and their children's lives. The women were used to having money doled out to them by their spouses, and their spouses were also financially unfaithful by hiding the amount of revenue that the women generated from their work. The women's opinions weren't considered when their spouses made financial decisions which affected the entire family. The women wanted to educate their daughters, who were left out of school when finances were tight so that their brothers could be educated. Alternately, the girls were taken out of school by their fathers, who didn't believe that girls deserved an education. The women wanted the security of knowing that they had money saved up for a rainy day—their husbands didn't know how much money they expected at the end of the year. Borrowing or taking out loans from the bank had an interest rate attached, which dissuaded many women from taking out loans unless they were truly needed. There was also a time limit to repay the loans or else they would face repercussions. The banking initiative let the women receive larger amounts of money in one lump sum at the end of the year, which would not have otherwise been possible.

Financial stability and freedom also meant that the women could feed and clothe their children, provide for their own needs without relying on or answering to someone else, and not be abused and financially manipulated by their spouses. Because of the group's success, the original members' daughters recognized that they could become women of change and eventually began their own group. Members of this group were able to chip in to pay their tuition when their parents were unable to. A few of the girls paid their way into vocational schools after graduating from primary school.

Stability and freedom relate to each other because both words provide assurance, hope, liberation, and a sense of self-worth. Having financial stability ensures that you have financial security, which in itself is freedom. This could eliminate the fear of not knowing how your basic needs will be met. Financial freedom means having no fear or coercion, so you can make the financial decisions you are comfortable with or that need to be made; that way you won't become destitute or be at another's mercy when you stand up for your rights.

The word *Oroko* means "welcome," and Oroko children are raised to be welcoming, warm, obedient, and respectful toward adults. When adults congregate, the children run errands while the adults deliberate and attend to business. As a child, whenever I was at my grandparents' while the women were meeting, I was the designated snack and water fetcher; the women would occasionally yell out, "Iya Makane, abeg bring me corn and groundnuts," and "Iya Makane, bring me wata for drink."

One day while I was busy bringing snacks from the kitchen to the living room, I heard the treasurer call out my name: "LaBelle Makane!" My heart skipped a beat before I heard Mom's response to my name: "Five thousand CFA francs!" The rest of the women clapped and cheered loudly—they usually clapped and cheered for each other when large amounts were saved as a form of encouragement. Mom added my name to the list of the women in the Oroko association. I was only nine years old.

I instantly become a member of the association just for banking purposes; I didn't attend the meetings or vote on any issues. Before Mom added my name to the association, I never thought that kids could save; I thought it was something only adults did. I learned from that day that even kids could save money—there is no age requirement to start. After that first day, every time my name was called and Mom shouted out the amount she saved for me, my heart swelled with pride. Even though I didn't understand the depth and implication of what Mom was teaching me, I knew it was very special. It made me realize how deeply she cared for me.

I later understood that it was important to save small amounts of money toward big purchases or events and to have money saved up for any eventualities. The money Mom saved for me was for boarding school after I graduated from primary school. Secondary schools, especially private ones, are considerably more expensive than primary schools. I was going to attend one of the most expensive girl's boarding schools in the country: Saker Baptist College. As a woman of change, Mom knew the power of financial independence in women and the importance of passing on that knowledge to the next generation. She taught me money management and saving skills, which paid off immensely. By the time I got to Saker, I was more conscious of money's value. I only spent my allowance, which I was given at the start of each trimester, and never asked for more until school was out. I was extremely careful and organized and guarded my possessions with care, knowing that they were purchased with hard-earned money.

By my third year in Saker, I was determined to earn my pocket money. Since my mother was in the United States and sent home lots of Avon products, which were rare in Cameroon and were in high demand, I asked her to send lots of roll-ons, body sprays, and lip glosses that I could sell to my school-mates to earn my allowance. I also saved some of my school allowance to spend during the holidays. I now realize Mom was teaching me that I was valuable, worthy, special, and de-serving of an education—that I should be self-reliant.

Financial literacy in the aspect of personal finances is not taught in schools in Cameroon like some schools in the US. Instead of learning about personal finances, Cameroonian students in economics and finance classes learn about the wealth and resources of the country, especially as it relates to the production and consumption of goods and services or the management of large sums of money by the government. Most children then learn about money and personal finances in an unconventional manner.

Due to the high level of financial abuse and financial in-fidelity that plagued African women, I believed that financial abuse was only a problem faced by African women. After moving to the United States, I soon found that this wasn't true. I've read and heard horror stories from women of dif-ferent ethnicities and races about the financial abuse that they suffer or have suffered in their marriages. I now know that many women in the world are stuck in bad relationships due to financial abuse and dependency.

During one of our sessions on financial literacy and wom-en's empowerment at the AGILE club, a Caucasian girl who visited the group a few times shared that finance was the most sensitive topic in her home. Her mother experienced financial abuse and financial infidelity in her marriage; the girl's father controlled the family's finances, manipulated and hid the bank account information, and doled out money to his wife as he saw fit. Whenever the girl's mother asked about their finances, the girl's father would retort,

"I have it covered. Do you know how to manage money?"

"I just want to know how much we have in each account so I don't worry," her mother timidly responded.

"Are you accusing me of something, after all I do for this family? Don't I take care of you and the children enough?" her father yelled.

"I'm sorry, I didn't mean anything by it," her mother apologized, dropping the topic.

That young lady was a senior in high school at the time and was determined not to become financially dependent on anyone or experience what her mother went through. The girl started working during her sophomore year and saved almost every penny she earned. Her goal was to be self-sufficient once she moved out, which her parents told her would be after high school. She was determined to find a roommate to split bills with as opposed to moving in with a boyfriend.

She went on to share tips with the other girls about how to start saving while in high school and also cautioned the girls about the dangers of staying in an abusive relationship just because the man has financial means. From that young lady's experience and my own, I now believe that if we start to teach girls about the importance of financial independence earlier, many of them will avoid abusive relationships. If girls are taught that they are whole and capable of taking care of themselves, they can enjoy stability and freedom and can avoid abusive relationships a lot sooner than if they believe they cannot make it without a man.

I once worked in retail with a hardworking, kind-hearted, and gentle Chinese woman, Ms. Juan, for six years. I got to know her pretty well and we had candid conversations whenever possible. I quickly realized that she had a pattern: she became antsy about ten minutes before the end of her shift, collecting her purse and lunch bag and placing them under a cash register. She would look at her watch repeatedly until it was time for her to leave, clocking out at the exact hour, then rush into the mall to pick up a day-old free newspaper for her husband. Since she walked with a limp and was already in her sixties, the limp became more apparent when she ran. She had to be outside of the store no later than five minutes after her shift or else her husband would be furious. He showed up every day at the exact time that her shift ended. He parked in front of the employee entrance, waiting impatiently in the car. I summoned up the courage once and asked her why she didn't drive.

"I never learned how to," she responded.

"But you've been in the United States for almost thirty years. Surely, you could have learned how to drive if you wanted to," I remarked.

"My husband thought getting two cars would be a waste of money. Besides, he brings me to and from work and takes me to the grocery store—he takes me to the important places."

"But Ms. Juan, didn't you ever want to drive?"

"I wanted to but my husband wouldn't allow it."

Sometimes during our breaks we would go window-shopping in the mall. She confessed that she wanted certain things but never purchased any of them. I didn't understand why she couldn't purchase something she truly wanted; after all, she worked very hard.

One payday, I overheard two ladies in Human Resources (HR) whispering about her. Her husband was sitting in the waiting area; as soon as she emerged, he scolded her in Mandarin in front of the HR ladies. She looked embarrassed and terrified but forced a smile as she signed for her check and handed it over to him. The HR ladies were furious and said that they wanted to shake some sense and respect into him. They referred to Ms. Juan as an abused woman—I suspected the same.

I also learned that Ms. Juan's husband only came into the store on payday. Ms. Juan would immediately hand him her check, and in turn he would give her twenty dollars of spending money—the only money she received every two weeks. I was enraged and saddened when I heard about her predicament and finally asked why she let her husband treat her so poorly.

"Ms. Juan, why do you give your paycheck to your husband? Why do you accept all of his shenanigans?" I asked.

She gave a dry laugh and said, "LaBelle, you should know better. You're African—we have similar cultures."

I pointed out that culture is a human construct that can be changed, and financial abuse isn't intrinsic to any culture; there are many Asian and African men who treat their women well. If we reject abuse and speak out against it, we could increase that number even more.

"Well LaBelle, you can say that now because you're in America—you've become Americanized. You couldn't speak that way if you were still in Africa."

"Ms. Juan, I was raised in a home where my grandfather didn't treat my grandmother poorly. He respected her and valued her opinions. She ran and managed the home, including the finances. My grandfather handed over his pension to my grandmother, because she managed the budget. He sent us to her whenever we needed money as kids. They made decisions together. My grandparents' relationship gave me a different view of the kind of relationships I want for myself. Have you ever thought of leaving?"

She told me that it's considered taboo in her culture for a woman to leave her marriage; a divorced woman is treated with disdain. Then she added, "Besides, even if I were to leave him, where would I go? I can't take care of myself."

"But you've worked for almost thirty years!" I exclaimed.

"True, but he manages our finances. I wouldn't know where to begin. You know, this is why I've told my two daughters not to marry Asian men. I don't want them to experience what I go through. I've told them to only marry white men—that way they will be treated well."

"Sorry to tell you this, Ms. Juan, but some white men treat women similarly or worse. Some men are abusive regardless of their race and ethnicity. Please tell your daughters to always maintain their sense of self and to remember that they're worthy and valuable. Advise them to never accept any form of abuse from any man, regardless of his race. Also, encourage your daughters to learn how to manage their finances and be independent. You know, it wouldn't be a bad idea if you stood up for yourself. You do all the chores, cook all the meals, and also earn money. You are more than an equal partner in your marriage. Stand up for yourself, girl!"

Ms. Juan laughed, "LaBelle, do you want him to kick me out of his house? Besides, I'm too old to start fighting now. I don't have the strength to challenge or change traditions and customs. This is the way it's been for centuries."

I was deeply saddened to hear how she was treated at home, yet felt powerless to help. I wondered why society makes it so easy for men to feel no responsibility, guilt, or shame for abusing women; instead, women feel like it's abominable to walk out on an abuser. I was disheartened to realize that Ms. Juan believed she didn't have what it took to be self-sufficient and independent, though she had worked for almost thirty years. According to the National Coalition Against Domestic Violence, many women who return to an abusive relationship cite their inability to deal with their finances as a major contributing factor, often enhanced by the abuser having all of the economic and social standing and complete control over the family finances.[5] I told Ms. Juan about what Mom and Mami Alice did to help the women in Bekondo gain financial independence, hoping it could give her some brilliant ideas.

Mami Alice and Mom did two important things for the women in their community:

1. They provided a way for women to unite and work together.
2. They helped a group of women become financially stable role models for future generations, which in turn combated financial dependency.

The women started to work on each other's farms during the planting and harvesting season, because it allowed them all to get their work taken care of; a few even went into business together. In Mami Alice and Mom's example, do you think it was likely that the original association members'

---

5   Nancy Salamone, "Domestic Violence and Financial Dependency," *Forbes*, September 2, 2010.

daughters would have started their own association without an example to follow? Perhaps, but not likely.

I know that not every girl is blessed to have female relatives who teach her about the importance of saving. If you don't have such role models within your family, all is not lost—there are many people around you who can help. Look at the women within your community, find a financially successful one, and ask her to be your mentor. You can also ask a financially savvy friend to teach you her tricks, or ask a financial expert at your local bank for help and guidance.

If you are already an empowered, financially savvy woman, there are simple things you can teach others:

- Live within your means: Teach someone else how to live within their means by example. For instance, show her how to create a list of all her income and expenses. Make sure her expenses are less than or equal to her income, but never above. Then, have her sit down and do it herself. Have her create her typical monthly list, then go through it and teach her how to differentiate between needs and wants.
- Earn money: Have a woman write down her skills and research how she can use them to earn money. For instance, she can list her skills on a freelance site such as Fiverr. If she is creative and makes sellable items such as jewelry or clothing, you can help her open an Etsy store online where her creations can be sold; she will get to be in charge of the pricing.
- Manage money: Help a woman keep track of her expenses by balancing her accounts monthly using the back of her checkbook. For instance, create a monthly budget or teach her how to save automatically. She can have her bank

withdraw a certain amount out of her regular account and deposit into an account with restrictions and penalties on withdrawal.

It's imperative for women to become financially independent and self-sufficient, because it raises morale and can stop them from feeling hopeless. Women are role models for their daughters and other young girls and should set a good example by being financially independent. With the rising cost of living, it's an added bonus for families when both parents earn money.

The association created many women of change who took their rightful places in the community. Some became business owners and combined forces with other women. One woman, Sister Terese Bume, used her savings from the association wisely, soared beyond the community's expectations, and became a pillar in the village. Sister Terese took advantage of the banking initiative, multiplied her savings, greatly improved her life, and became an inspiration to others. Uneducated and unmarried, Sister Terese had two goals in life: to become financially stable and to educate her nieces. She rented a two-bedroom apartment from my grandparents and soon became a part of our family. She made a living selling *corn chaff* (a meal of corn and beans) every morning and worked on her farm in the afternoons.

After she received her first savings from the association, my grandparents gave her permission to extend her apartment's veranda and turn it into a modest diner. Her business exploded when she added a Cameroonian delicacy, *fufu and eru*, to the menu. Eventually, her earnings multiplied and she doubled her yearly savings. At the end of each year, she left a percentage of her savings in the bank, which gave her a head start at the beginning of the next year. She bought two more cocoa farms, hired employees, educated her nieces, gave loans to others, and ultimately built a bigger house for herself and moved out of my grandparents' property.

Two other women from the association went into business together since they couldn't afford the cost of starting individual businesses. They sold *okrika* (secondhand clothing and shoes) at the market by renting one of Mom's stalls. Before this banking initiative, only men owned the few clothing stores that existed. Another woman, who was an apprentice to a male tailor and often complained about how poorly he treated her, eventually bought a sewing machine with her savings and started her own business.

When women come together, they realize that their similarities are greater than their differences and that every woman is fighting a battle. They realize that they're capable of overcoming anything if they work together. Financial insecurities brought the Oroko women of Bekondo together to find solutions to their problems, take control over their lives, and become each other's allies. Everyone in the community felt the positive changes and impacts that the association made in these women's lives, and the community was better off because of them. As the gender pay gap remains stagnant all over the world, coupled with the other practices that hold women back from achieving their full potentials, women and men of change need to create opportunities that allow women financial stability; to make the kind of impact they are capable of making. Our finances are the lifeblood of everything we want to do.

TAKEAWAYS

- Create a safe haven: Form a sisterhood. Make a space for yourself and the women around you where you can help each other.

- Become a mentor to other women and girls: Be aware of your influence on younger women. Regardless of status, we all have benefited from the help of powerful women who provided support and guidance when we needed it.

- Collaborate and network: Combine forces with another woman or women by bringing your skills and talents together and creating a mutually beneficial opportunity. For instance, start a business with other women, work on a project with other women, and invest in another woman's idea.

- Save money: It's possible to save money with little or no financial knowledge—ask a financially savvy person for guidance.

- Read something about money every day: When you read about money, you begin to understand global economics. Suze Orman is a financial guru who gives practical money advice—read her blog or follow her on Twitter.

- Another insightful financial guru who gives practical steps on how to attain financial stability is bestselling author Dennis Kimbro, who writes not only on ways to achieve financial freedom but also on how to break generational poverty among underdeveloped countries and the methods by which impoverished black Americans can pull themselves out of poverty and reach their full potential.

- Know the difference between financial infidelity and financial abuse in a relationship. Financial infidelity is when your partner keeps you ignorant about your finances or hides money and assets from you. Financial abuse is when your spouse has complete control of the finances, limits your access to bank accounts, doles out money to you, and picks a fight every time finances are brought up.

- Achieve economic success: Be in control of your life and be an example to your children.

DISCUSSION QUESTIONS

- Write down two of your strongest skills and share with the group. Listen to each other's skills, brainstorm to find out which skills complement each other, and collaborate using those skills.

- Write down any vision, investment, or business idea you have. Share with the group to find networking partners or to get ideas about how to move forward.

- What are your weekly practices surrounding money? Do you read about it? Talk about it with family, friends, or financial experts? What do you do to ensure you are financially savvy? Share with a friend.

- Have you ever created a SMART goal (S = Specific, M = Measurable, A = Achievable, R = Relevant, and T = Time bound) for a major purchase or investment? How did you ensure you followed through with the four stages? Share with a friend.

- Have you ever experienced financial abuse and/or financial infidelity in your relationship? How did it manifest itself? How did you recognize it? What did you do about it? Discuss with a friend.

- Being independent is liberating and empowering. What are three ways you live independently in your relationship? How about in your career?

KEY WORDS

Sisterhood

Empower

Self-worth

Accountability

Financial abuse

Value

Pioneer

Financial infidelity

Self-sufficient

Collaboration

Financial literacy

SMART goals

Investment

Courageous

Educate

CHAPTER TWO

THE COMMUNAL BENEFITS OF EDUCATED WOMEN

Here's to strong women!
May we know them.
May we be them.
May we raise them.
—Unknown

December 2013 was the first time I visited Cameroon since I'd left in August 2000. I was filled with nostalgia by the thought of going home after so many years; I couldn't wait to get back to familiar sights, sounds, smells, and faces. I decided to use my vacation to empower women and girls—to let them know that they're capable of greatness and have the power to make positive changes in their lives, regardless of what society tells them. In my search for a group to work with, I came across a nonprofit for teen mothers, Teenage Mothers' Institute, and was immediately captivated by its motto: "A social venture incubator for girls and young women to discover their own potential as change agents," a theme so dear to my heart. I was blown away by this initiative, since most teen mothers in Africa (and around the world) are shunned by family members and society; they're judged harshly and considered failures.

I contacted the center and was given permission to speak with the girls. Favour, the youth worker, cautioned me not to get my hopes up; she explained how difficult it is to track down each girl during the holidays. The girls use the holiday free time to earn money doing various odd jobs.

We stopped at the organization's main office, where the girls are taught basic computer skills and given lessons on sexually transmitted infections, HIV/AIDS, and teen pregnancy prevention, among other topics. The executive director told me about the center's enormous financial challenges, even though it cost less than one hundred dollars for some of the girls to complete a certification course or to get their high schools diplomas. He asserted that donors are needed year-round, because the center is incredibly important to the community. Not all the young girls who benefit from the center are teen mothers, and none of the girls who attend the center to learn basic computer skills and other topics are turned away.

To my pleasant surprise, when we got to the center there were eighteen girls already waiting, some with their babies on their backs. Most of the girls had walked in flip-flops on stony roads for over thirty minutes in the hot sun and canceled their plans when they learned that a woman from the United States was eager to speak with them.

I started off with an icebreaker activity. I asked each girl to share her biggest dream with the group—what she would love to be in the future, if given the opportunity. I was moved to tears once the girls started to share their dreams, because I immediately noticed a pattern in their responses: they were selfless!

The oldest girl in the group, who had a high school diploma, was the first to speak:

"Miss, I want to become a teacher. I want to make school fun for little children—I want them to enjoy learning. When I was younger, I didn't like school. My teachers were wicked. They called me a 'dull girl' every time I didn't answer a question correctly. They told me I better become smart because I'm not as beautiful as the other girls who will get husbands. I always felt dumb."

"Miss, I want to become a doctor. I want to open a free clinic so the poor people and their children in my community can see a doctor when sick," said another.

"Miss, I want to become a businesswoman. I want to own a very big store that would carry everything the people in my community need. I would pay people in my community to work in the store. I want to provide a better life for my parents, brothers, and sisters, and to someday be able to send my children to school—all the way to university."

I was touched by their selflessness and thoughtfulness. The girls also created a sisterhood and support system: they woke each other up every morning by walking over to each other's homes and knocking on the doors. They made the one-hour walk to the center in pairs or in a group, because walking alone makes it easier for girls to give up and go back home if harassed by men. They'd also help each other babysit. Listening to the girls reinforced what I already knew: when a girl is empowered, a community is empowered. These girls were becoming women of change by watching out for themselves and their sisters. They only needed guidance and opportunities to become their best selves.

At the end of my presentation, I received a long round of applause with loud cheers and a standing ovation. One of the girls ran from the back of the room waving a bill in the air, which prompted more cheers from the others. She gave me a big hug and placed a 1,000 CFA note (equivalent to two dollars) on the table in front of me and made a speech:

"Miss, the speech you just made deserves a million dollars. Unfortunately, we don't have that kind of money to give to you; you will make a speech for a million dollars someday."

The others continued yelling, clapping, and thanking me. They encouraged her to go on with her speech:

"Miss, thank you so much for taking time out of your holidays to motivate and encourage us; it tells us we matter. What you just did has never been done for us by anyone before. Since we are girls, we're not thought highly of by anyone, not even by our parents. Our parents encourage our brothers to pursue an education and would do anything to give them one. They encourage us to get married instead. Miss, some of the men who ask for our hands in marriage are old, have children, or are already married. I'm one of the few girls who attend this center who isn't a teenage mom. I come to the center to learn computer skills and the other courses they teach. I want to be somebody in the future; we all want to be somebody. We know the only way for us to make something of ourselves is to seize every educational opportunity available to us. You've just made us believe we can actually become successful and independent someday. Thank you and God bless you."

She placed the money in my hands—an amount that means little or nothing to most, but could provide dinner to a poor struggling family in Cameroon. I was moved to tears. While the girls and their kids snacked on the treats I provided, I took pictures and got to know the girls individually. I spoke with two beautiful and intelligent young women:

"Miss, our lives are so hard and we need a break. Please take us with you to America. We promise we'll be no trouble at all. We'll cook, clean your home, do your laundry, and do your chores. All we need in return is an education."

While I was explaining the adoption process to the girls, the oldest girl approached us with her two kids.

"Excuse me, Miss, can I talk to you alone?"

I moved to the side with her but was still within earshot of the other two girls.

"Miss, first off, I want to apologize for having two kids I can't properly take care of. Once I got pregnant the first time, I should have learned from that, but I went ahead and made the same mistake. Everyone says I'm a disappointment, I deserve my suffering, and no man will ever marry me with two kids. I'm so sorry."

I was alarmed by the unmerited apology and quickly stopped her. I assured her that I wasn't judging her and that she didn't owe me or anyone else an apology. I also advised her to not refer to her children as mistakes, and to attend the center's health classes about how to avoid sexually transmitted infections and unwanted pregnancies until she was financially able to provide for kids. I further assured her that she was not a failure and deserved great things. She immediately gave a sigh of relief, but I could tell she was heavily burdened.

"Miss, all I want is to go to a teacher's training college. I don't have the money to pay for it—I don't have help. If you know anyone who can help me, that would be a blessing. I must take the kids home now. Thank you for coming to speak with us."

She started to walk away and the other two girls immediately rushed over. I assumed they wanted to pick up the conversation where we left off, and was stunned by what they said next:

"Miss, if you can do anything for any one of us, please do it for Stella. She needs all the help she can get. She wakes up every day at five in the morning and prepares a meal of *koki* (a pudding made from beans tied in plantain leaves) and plantains. By nine she is out the door with the tray of food on her head, the youngest child tied to her back, and holding the older kid by the hand. She goes hawking from one neighborhood to the next all day. At times we see her walking in the hot afternoon with her kids; she rarely takes a break. When we see them, we offer them water and food if we have some. You see, her first child is four and is due to start primary school next year. She's determined to send her daughter to school. Tell everyone you know about the center so that they can become donors. We need support."

I was speechless and looked at the girls in awe. Never before had I encountered such genuinely compassionate and loving souls. This truly was a sisterhood. Each of the girls needed help and had unique challenges, yet they still advocated for one another. Once I got back to Minnesota, I wrote about the experience and published it on my blog, LinkedIn, and Facebook, calling on people to support the center. I saved the money that the young woman gave me as memorabilia. It reminds me that, as an empowered woman and a change agent, it's my duty to motivate and inspire the women and girls around me, as well as the next generation.

As an empowered, educated woman, I spend most of my working hours talking to young girls and women about the value of education. If more educated women become women of change and take active roles in promoting girls' education in any way possible, especially in areas where girls are heavily marginalized and kept out of school, there could be a huge shift in thinking and development. Nothing excites me more than coming across women who got their education and have become inspirational advocates to other women against all odds. I enjoy listening to their stories of perseverance; we speak candidly about how educated women can create long-lasting effects by becoming champions for women and girls' education. I came across the next woman's story on social media—she got her education against great odds but is now a beacon for the positive power of girls' education. I was intrigued when I learned that we have a similar background, as she is from Cameroon.

HILDA BIH

Hilda Bih is a fascinating young lady with a big heart and a bigger personality. She has faced and continues to face daily tough challenges—more than most of us ever will in our lifetimes. Despite her struggles, she's a fighter and doesn't let adversity affect her zeal to keep thriving. Hilda was born in Bamenda, in the Northwest Region of Cameroon, the second of nine children from a very modest but loving family. Her mother was a seamstress and her father was a taxi driver. Despite their limited finances, her parents ensured that each of their children would live up to their full potential by getting an education.

Hilda was just like any ordinary child growing up—curious, energetic, and jovial. By age four, it was apparent that something was wrong with her health. She had difficulty performing simple tasks like walking and holding onto objects. Her symptoms worsened as she got older; her parents panicked and took her to multiple hospitals. Unfortunately, due to the poor medical system and inadequate training, none of the doctors could diagnose her ailment. After visiting with many doctors, herbalists, and faith healers to no avail, the family turned to witch doctors. The witch doctors accused certain family members of causing her body's weakness and immobility. They put Hilda through rigorous regimens where herbs and mysterious animal bones were used to painfully massage her body, after which she would soak in foul odors for days at a time. When Hilda didn't get better, the witch doctors accused her of being a child from the spirit world, a "witch child." This label alienated her family from the neighbors.

Her parents reluctantly accepted her disability and helped her with daily activities. The rest of her immediate family and some of her extended family members eventually made the necessary adjustments to make her life less stressful.

Going to school was difficult, since there weren't special accommodations for disabled children. Hilda persisted, knowing that getting an education was the only way she could live up to her full potential and become financially independent, especially growing up in a society heavily influenced by patriarchal norms. The few self-sufficient women she had seen were those who had some form of education.

During the early stages of her disease, she could walk slowly to and from school, albeit with difficulty and pain. However, as the disease progressed and she lost more mobility, family members had to carry her on their backs. At age ten, she befriended Maureen, a schoolmate her age. Maureen became an ally and a devoted friend. She carried Hilda on her back to and from school every day and never once complained.

At fourteen, Hilda got a tricycle and rode to school with great difficulty. She was too big for people to carry on their backs, but she was uncompromising about her education. She also developed a special shorthand technique of taking notes to keep up with the other students. Though she was bullied at times, Hilda persisted, excelled at school, and became incredibly resilient.

She attributes her tenacity to her parents' love and devotion. Their encouragement, support, care, and determination to provide her with an education despite their limited resources made her believe she was smart and worthy of accomplishing great things. Hilda's biggest strength came from a lesson she learned in Sunday school about God's love and how all are created in His/Her image. This lesson reinforced that neither her gender nor her disability made her inferior to anyone else.

Hilda is a trailblazer. She became a journalist with the Cameroon Radio Television Bamenda branch, making her one of the few journalists in the country with a physical disability. Recognizing the plight of the disabled in Cameroon, she uses her platform to draw attention to the disabled community's needs.

She encourages parents of disabled children to provide them with an education. While she was fortunate, most children with disabilities are kept out of school. Disabilities are commonly believed to be caused by a supernatural force or curse, which causes others to shun the disabled out of fear and ignorance. Disabled children are also kept out of school because it's assumed that they are too slow to learn, so an education would be wasted on them. Hilda shared a story of a disabled woman whose only dream was to become an entrepreneur, but she was abandoned by her family in an institution for years. This woman reached out to Hilda and they worked diligently to start up her business. Today, that woman runs her own business, lives independently, and provides employment for other community members. Hilda notes that life is harder for disabled women in Cameroon, because they face the risk of being raped and assaulted while living on the streets.

As a woman of change, Hilda is also a champion of girls' and women's education. She knows the best way to break the wheel of female inferiority is by empowering women through education to become employable and creative, and to develop a sense of worth. She founded an organization, the ESTHER Project (named after Hilda's favorite Bible character), that empowers and mentors women and girls using uplifting principles from the Bible. The project raises funds to provide scholarships for the women and girls it serves by forging partnerships with educational organizations. Hilda asserts that women throughout history have been deprived of opportunities and it's time to right this wrong. We all must join together in female empowerment in order to achieve equality and make a tremendous impact on the world's economy.

Hilda was finally diagnosed with muscular dystrophy in 2014, thanks to the Speak Foundation. While attending a conference in the United States, Hilda was tested and diagnosed after over twenty years of moving between hospitals. Her muscles get weaker as she gets older, yet she continues to fight for marginalized people. She recently began drawing and painting pictures with her mouth due to losing mobility in her hands. "I find pleasure in drawing and painting beautiful pictures. I enjoy inspiring others and adding color to the world," she explains.

Hilda's personal experiences and accomplishments clearly demonstrate the incredible power education has to change not only the course of a woman's life but the lives of others in her community. Hilda asserts that belief in herself combined with resilience, perseverance, determination, and education has paid off. These qualities are some of the most important attributes women need to navigate, survive, and thrive in an unjust world.[6]

In their book *Now, Discover Your Strengths*, Marcus Buckingham and Donald O. Clifton state that every person is capable of doing something better than the next 10,000 people. They

---

6 Marcus Buckingham & Donald O. Clifton, *Now, Discover Your Strengths* (New York: The Free Press, 2001), # 25-30

call this area your strength zone. John Maxwell writes, "It's been my observation that people can increase their ability in an area by only two points on a scale from one to ten. For example, if your natural talent in an area is four, with hard work you may raise it to a six. In order words, you can go from a little below average to a little above average. But let's say you find a place where you are a seven; you have the potential to become a nine, maybe even a ten, if it's your strength zone and you work hard! That helps you advance from one in ten thousand talent to one in one hundred thousand talent, but only if you do the other things needed to maximize your talent."

In my zeal to connect and engage more with women who achieved their education amidst great challenges, I became friends with another speaker while taking a course at the Minnesota Speaker Academy. This fascinating lady is passionate about women's education and encourages women to develop their natural talents to compete within their strength zone.

MARCIA MALZAHN

Marcia Malzahn was born and raised in Nicaragua; her father was an attorney and composer, and her mother was a home-maker. Marcia is the second of six children and grew up in an upper-class family with maids and luxury. She describes her childhood as fun and happy. As a child, she enjoyed telling stories and playing with numbers; she always played as the bank when the family played Monopoly. Her parents sent their children to the best schools and inculcated them a love for learning within them.

At age thirteen, Marcia's peaceful, happy, sheltered life was changed forever. Her family fled from Nicaragua just two weeks before the Communist party launched a military effort against the regime of longtime dictator Anastasio Somoza DeBayle, whose family ruled the country from 1937 until they were ousted in 1979. The Malzahn family's escape was nothing short of a miracle; they got seats on a Red Cross cargo plane that made an emergency stop in Nicaragua just to pick up Salvadorans who lived in Nicaragua. While the pilot was out attending to other duties, Marcia's father snuck their twenty-five pieces of luggage onto the cargo plane. When the pilot returned and found extra luggage in the plane, Marcia's father struck a deal—he bargained to exchange a piece of luggage for a family member. Eventually all their luggage was taken out, which created just enough space for seven family members. One person had to be left behind and Marcia's father decided it should be him.

The family tearfully parted ways and wondered if they

would ever see each other again. Miraculously, one last plane heading to Costa Rica from Argentina made an emergency stop in Nicaragua that same day and had one empty seat. Marcia's father got on the plane and headed to Costa Rica. Two weeks after their separation, the father reunited with the rest of his family in El Salvador, where they were hosted by Marcia's mother's sister (who lived there).

Her family eventually moved from El Salvador to the Dominican Republic, where they lived with their father's sister for two months. Two and a half months after they moved into their own apartment, everything they had was destroyed by Hurricane David. There was no water or electricity for four months. Marcia, only fourteen at the time, started to wonder if the misery would ever end.

Marcia's family soon experienced major financial setbacks because her father couldn't practice law in the Dominican Republic. He eventually became an insurance agent. Her mother, who had always been a stay-at-home mom, became an entrepreneur by making jewelry. She worked tirelessly night and day and ultimately opened a jewelry store. Marcia watched her mother in awe and was motivated by her tenacity to work harder at school. Her family stayed in the Dominican Republic for seven years, during which Marcia completed high school and a year of college. The family then traveled to the United States with the help of her mother's business.

When Marcia got to Minnesota, she was eager and anxious to mix into the melting pot. Like most newly arrived immigrants, she had a strong accent and drew negative attention from the community. She thought her accent was a liability and worked hard to lose it. She eventually started to forget Spanish before her mother made her to realize the advantages of being bilingual.

As a Latina, Marcia was encouraged to go into the hospitality and cleaning industry. However, she wanted to follow her dreams by continuing her education. She was encouraged to become a bank teller due to her love of numbers. She saw this opportunity as a step closer to her dream of becoming a banker—working with numbers and managing funds. To stay ahead, she studied the required software and knew all about not only her position but other positions at the bank. She soon became the go-to woman at work. Due to her dedication, knowledge, and commitment to her job and her love for learning, she advanced from a teller to a manager and eventually to higher management.

As an executive woman in a typically male-dominated profession, she was often the lone woman attending executive meetings with older Caucasian males. She was patronized and spoken down to during conferences and trainings: "Are we too hard on you, dear? Are we moving too fast for you? Can you keep up with the rest of us?"

Marcia didn't like to be patronized and always stood up for herself. She was able to compete with the best and brightest in the banking industry by operating within her strength zone and also getting an education to hone her skills. She continued to excel in her field and broke a few glass ceilings. Her biggest achievement was when her former boss asked her to help him start a new bank, which Marcia later became the president of. She was disheartened to learn that there were only ten female bank presidents in the Twin Cities when she took that position. She calls for young women with a knack for numbers to get an education in banking or finance in order to increase the gender representation in this industry.

As a woman of change, Marcia believes it's our duty to fight for women's educational rights: "As empowered women, it's our responsibility to pass on the knowledge we have acquired to other women. All women need some form of education so the next generation will be better off. We need to remind one another of how powerful, valuable, smart, and incredible we truly are. Together we are unstoppable—we matter."

As an author, speaker, and entrepreneur, Marcia has created a ministry for women entitled "Know Your Value." She says that it's imperative for women to know their value, which in turn will guide them in the direction they want their lives to take. Marcia's goal is to help other women to become successful, not only in their careers, but in every aspect of their lives; to be whole.

In her book, *The Fire Within*, Marcia helps women connect their gifts with their calling. She has extended her mission overseas and spoken at an international women's leadership conference in Kigali, Uganda, where she encouraged the women to get any form of education in order to become better leaders and role models for the young girls in their communities. She has gone back to Nicaragua a few times over thirty years and had the honor of giving her presentation in Spanish for the first time to the working women of Nicaragua. The visit also gave her ideas of ways she could continue to empower, promote, and support education for women in her native country and all over the world.

These women confirm what I already know: any form of education is the most powerful tool to break the cycle of inferiority that women experience because of their gender. Education not only gives women the ammunition they need to become self-reliant, employable, and confident and to break out of poverty, but also changes the way women view themselves, opens a new world of possibilities, and allows women to make genuine choices about the kinds of lives they wish to lead. This old adage sums up the benefits that society enjoys when women are given equal opportunities:

"Give a man a fish and he eats for a day. Teach a man to fish and he eats for a lifetime. But teach a woman to fish, and everyone eats for a lifetime."

An article in *Inside Philanthropy* states that there are approximately sixty-two million girls between the ages of six and fifteen who aren't in school. The article lists a few facts about the benefits of investing in women's education: If all women had at least a primary education, an estimated 1.7 million children would be protected from stunting and malnutrition. That number jumps to twelve million if all women had a secondary education. If all girls completed primary school, it would result in 14 percent fewer child marriages. It's estimated that a one-point increase in girls' education results in a 0.3 percentage point average increase in gross domestic product.[7]

Feeling inferior leaves women doubting their own abilities; women are afraid of making certain decisions that their families and society could benefit from, due to feeling like they aren't qualified to make such decisions. This leaves many things in society undone or unaccomplished, as half of the population is conditioned to feel inferior and not invested in. This ultimately slows the growth and development of each country.

---

7   Sue-Lynn Moses, "A Case Study in the Power of Film: Why a Doc on Girls Pulled in Big Bucks," *Inside Philanthropy*, August 4, 2016.

TAKEAWAYS

- To break the cycle of female inferiority, you need to know where your skills and talents lie, be brave, and seek learning opportunities.

- Seize every opportunity presented to you and make the most of it.

- Regardless of the challenges you face, know that you were created for a purpose.

- Always follow your intuition. It's extremely important to trust your gut. Psychologists posit that the unconscious mind dictates decision-making more than we think. It's also vital to follow your intuition because it's shaped by your past experiences and the existing knowledge you've gained from them.

- Be determined and persistent when going after your dreams. Don't allow anything or anyone to distract you from your path.

DISCUSSION QUESTIONS

- In my network marketing group we say, "If your dream doesn't make you cry then it isn't big enough." Write down what you believe your purpose is. Share with a friend and ask her to do the same.

- What are three ways you achieve complete balance in your work, career, ambition, self, and personal life without neglecting certain aspects? Share with a friend and have her do the same.

- What are some things you do to build self-confidence? Share with a friend and have her do the same.

- Take a strength-finder test to start operating within your strength zone and grow. Share your findings with others.

- Have you ever been ostracized? How did you handle the situation? Discuss with a group.

KEY WORDS

Incubator

Sisterhood

Trailblazer

Self-discovery

Compassion

Advocate

Education

Empathy

Strength zone

Self-sufficient

Purpose

Phenomenal

Donors

Fate

Life balance

THE PATRIARCHY

In all twelve major religions in the world—
Christianity, Islam, Hinduism, Buddhism, Baha'i,
Judaism, Confucianism, Jainism, Shinto, Sikhism,
Taoism, and Zoroastrianism—god is male.

CHAPTER THREE

WOMEN'S WORTH IN SOCIETY; YOU ARE WHOLE AND COMPLETE

Men don't age better than women,
they're just allowed to age.
—Anonymous, popularized by Carrie Fisher

One night after working on a presentation for International Women's Day 2014, I picked up a little devotional, a birthday gift from my dear friend Amy Long. As I opened the book, I came across a story we were told several times as children. The memories of how I felt when I heard that story as a child came flooding back. Here's the story:

In most African cultures many years ago, the standard price for a bride was two healthy, well-fed cows. Not many men could afford two cows at once, so it was an honor to be able to do so. When a man wanted to marry a young woman, he told her family his intentions. If the family thought he was suitable for their daughter, they agreed to the marriage after the man paid the price of two healthy cows.

In a village lived a plain woman who was described

as ugly by the villagers. It was customary for the oldest daughter to be married off first, but it was the opposite in the case of this woman: her three beautiful younger sisters had been married off with their bride prices completely paid. Her parents began to worry that their oldest daughter would never get married; the village marriage maker had never asked about her marital status. In desperation, her parents announced that they would pay up to four cows to any man who would marry their plain daughter. After this publicity, the woman became the laughingstock of the village, who said, "She's so ugly that her family has to pay for a man to marry her!"

One day, a stranger appeared at the woman's parents' door and offered to pay eight cows for her. Her father was bewildered since she was above the marrying age. Because her father was full of integrity, he wanted the man to see his daughter first before making an offer, but the man declined, to spare the woman further embarrassment. Everyone was perplexed by the stupidity of a man who would pay eight cows for such an ugly woman. The next day, they were married and the plain woman left home as a bride. As was to be expected, many beautiful women were hurt and quarreled with their husbands, asking, "Wasn't I worth eight cows to you?" The plain woman's marriage thrived, and she was never sent back home.

After many years, the story of the bride with eight cows became a legend. A new village story teller (griot) searched for the couple to see how the marriage had fared. After walking for many days, he came to the couple's home. He knocked at the door and was greeted by a woman. He asked if he was at the home of the man who had paid eight cows for his bride; the woman said yes. He then asked to speak with her husband, whom he asked:

"For the record, why did you do it?"

"Didn't my wife let you into the house?" the husband asked.

"Yes, your beautiful wife let me in," the griot replied.

"Well then, didn't you think she was worth even ten cows?" challenged the husband.

"Yes. But I'm not questioning why you would pay eight cows for a beautiful woman. I've traveled this distance to understand why you paid eight cows for an ugly woman."

The husband was silent for a while and then called for his wife. The very beautiful and gracious woman entered the room. The man told the griot,

"This is my only wife. She's the one I paid eight cows for, and I would gladly pay eight more."

"They said she was ugly!" the griot exclaimed.

"She was never ugly," the husband said. "Her beauty is on the inside, never shown on her face. Before we got married, she was simply a reflection of what she was told. They called her ugly and she behaved in response. But eight cows made a huge difference in how she thought of herself. In all our land, that amount has never been paid for another woman."

When we heard this story as children, I was rooting for this poor, plain lady. I wanted her to get a husband so her self-worth could be validated; so she would be complete. I was ecstatic when she eventually got a husband! But when I read this story as a grown woman, I was shocked and appalled. I realized that women have been conditioned to believe that we aren't complete in our own rights—that marriage is our greatest achievement and that having a man validates our existence. The story also showed me that women are sometimes considered property, and marriage is for a woman's honor and a man's convenience. If the man is no longer satisfied with the woman, she is sent back home. The story also endorses and normalizes polygamy: the *griot* assumed that the lady who answered the door was the man's beautiful wife and still expected to see an ugly wife.

The truth is, when girls hear these stories, they learn that they are weak, fragile, and incomplete without a man. Girls are told that they should focus on being beautiful, pure, and domesticated and see other women as competition. On the contrary, when boys hear these stories, they learn that they are leaders—strong, independent—and need to be decisive, adventurous, and hardworking to be successful.

Even though we are in a different era from when this story was first told, these ideologies are still promoted and women are still validated by these themes. Women and young girls are bombarded daily regarding their self-worth through various sources, the most prominent being the media. In the United States, we are constantly surrounded by the media and we eventually construct our identities through the media images we see. For instance, television shows, music videos, movies, social media, ads, magazines, and books promote women's worth through certain beauty standards. For instance, the show *The Swan* was all about women who were deemed ugly getting extreme makeovers, getting plastic surgery to compete in a beauty pageant. *Bridalplasty* showed twelve brides competing to undergo plastic surgery and achieve their desired look before winning a dream wedding. A show like *Fashion*

Police is all about what's trending in the fashion world; celebrity fashion styles are dissected, but physical appearances (especially of female celebrities) are often scrutinized. These beauty standards have drastic impacts on young women and their body images. Most young women strive to achieve the ideal beauty standards to the detriment of their health, believing that their looks determine their self-worth.

Women and girls also receive messages about their worth through relationships. In most communities, women in relationships are treated and spoken to differently than single women. In my community, for instance, once a girl gets married, she is rarely addressed by her name because that is considered disrespectful; she is addressed as Mrs. or Madame. If a man is vulgar or disrespectful to a woman, the general response from community members is, "Na man ei woman dat. No talk for ei so," pointing out that he is dealing with a man's wife—as though it is okay to be discourteous to a woman as long as she isn't married. Songs of praises are sung about women who are good cooks, keep a clean house, are gentle, and cater to a man's every need. In the United States, companies give preference to married women over single women; they're considered first for vacations, time off, and even get tax benefits. All of these messages tell women harmful things:

Women are valued when they are beautiful
Women are sexual objects[8]
Women are valued when they are domestic and passive
Other women are competition

---

8   Eileen Zurbriggen et al., *Report of the APA Task Force on the Sexualization of Girls* (Washington, DC: American Psychological Association, 2007).

In America, we're told similar stories by our families, schools, employers, religious institutions, media. Take, for example, the common commercial trope where a husband in housekeeping chaos is saved by his wife, who is immediately able to clean the kitchen and rescue the children hanging from the chandelier. The woman is shown that her worth lies in her ability to keep a clean house and manage the children. Another example can be found in superstar Beyoncé's pregnancies. There were intense debates and accusations that she didn't carry her own child during her first pregnancy; every video she appeared in after announcing she was pregnant was analyzed to prove that she was not truly pregnant. She was accused of putting on a prosthetic tummy while she used a surrogate so as not to destroy her figure. Her accusers insinuated that she was not enough of a woman to take on this duty—she was shamed for prioritizing her career over a feminine destiny. Whether or not this accusation is true is beside the point; it shows that even a successful businesswoman like Beyoncé is subject to her worth being tied to motherhood. She was likely affected by this accusation, which may have led to her publicizing obvious, stomach-baring photos in her second pregnancy.

Our worth is subtly tied to our ability to be good wives and mothers, yet we're given conflicting messages about it also being tied to successful careers and independence. For instance, a new Swiffer commercial shows a mom dressed for work and wearing heels, yet she picks up a mop and cleans up her son's mess on the floor before heading out. In most African homes, even in the United States, women are expected to do the cooking even after working a twelve-hour shift. When African men cook, they hide it from their peers to avoid being called a woman; alternately, the women hide their husband's cooking from others to avoid being shamed by family, friends, and community members for being a bad wife. These concepts don't work well together, because partners need to equally manage the family responsibilities, yet women's worth is often judged upon their success in managing a career and a household. This leads women to a lifetime of juggling, multitasking, and feeling as though they are constantly failing in certain aspects of their lives. Clearly, as these stories show, not even a woman like Beyoncé is immune to the impact of these expectations on the way women view themselves.

The patriarchy's global influence convinces women that their worth is tied to their physical beauty, which is followed by marriage and motherhood. Growing up, I was often told by girlfriends that I was lucky because I was pretty, and that I wouldn't have any issues getting married. In my early twenties a close friend chastised me often for not being wild and adventurous. She constantly remarked that if she were as pretty and skinny as I she would date all the men with fancy cars, knowing fully well she would gain a bad reputation but that her looks would more than make up for her reputation—she would still have men asking to marry her. She always concluded these lectures with a "LaBelle, you are wasting your looks." My female friends, my allies, were helping me tie my self-worth to my beauty and my ability to find a man.

When is society going to accept that not every woman wants to get married and have children, and that some women want to adopt rather than have biological children? When are we going to accept that some women truly desire children but can't have any for medical reasons? Why should a woman feel like a lesser human being if she chooses not to get married, and cannot or chooses not to have children? I abhor these patriarchal influences and ideologies, as society doesn't give single, childless men in their forties the grief it gives women. Don't get me wrong, it can be good for a woman to have a partner in her life, just as it is good for a man to have a partner in his life. Companionship can be an essential part of our existence, but it should be beneficial for both parties—we shouldn't look down on those who choose to live life differently from how society expects them to.

As women of change, we have to challenge this notion by not looking down on or discriminating against our unmarried and childless sisters. We have to stand up and speak out when our sisters are mocked or disrespected for not having the stereotypical lifestyle, and we should recognize the hurt that they suffer from this discrimination.

The stories we were told as children were devoid of positive female characters— they only had negative, nagging women. As a child, I was skeptical about trusting other women even though I was surrounded by inherently good ones. Every time I got closer to other girls, I wondered when they would bite me like a snake; I thought I was foolish for trusting women in spite of the stories I grew up with. When I read stories such as "Cinderella," just as in the African folktales, I noticed that the kind-hearted female characters were presented as good witches or had extraordinary powers. I wondered if ordinary women were capable of goodness. When men were mentioned in the stories, they appeared as good and kind heroes. At a young age, I started to believe that men were kind, trustworthy, and decent human beings, whereas women were not. At some point in my adolescence, I began to question why I was born a girl; I wanted to be a member of the cool and kind gender.

KATHLEEN RAGAN

Four years ago, I found an interesting book in a high school English literature classroom: *Fearless Girls, Wise Women and Beloved Sisters*. I was intrigued after reading the synopsis and immediately ordered a copy to read. The author, Kathleen Ragan, recognized some of the issues that I uncovered as an adult from the stories we were fed as children; Kathleen understood the responsibility to challenge those prescribed ideas.

Kathleen started reading bedtime stories to her year-old daughter, like many parents do, and was ecstatic when her daughter was old enough to appreciate the stories. Kathleen gathered all her favorite childhood books and started reading them, expecting her daughter to enjoy the books as much as Kathleen had as a child. To her dismay, Kathleen became increasingly uncomfortable reading one story after the other; she immediately recognized a pattern that made her uneasy, a trend she had not paid attention to as a child: there were virtually no female characters in the books, yet there was a predominance of male protagonists. Kathleen changed the pronouns from male to female. When there were female protagonists in stories, they were presented as negative characters: "A nagging mother-in-law who makes life intolerable even for the devil, a woman who personifies the misery in the world, or women who allow themselves to be mutilated by loved ones. Secondary characters like the wicked witch and stepmother abound."[9] Kathleen was horrified to realize the effects these stories would have on her daughter and other girls, both as children and as grown women.

As a mother, editor, and author, these stories that portrayed women and girls as helpless, evil, passive, or weak compelled Kathleen to go on a quest. She plunged deep into libraries, hunting for stories that portrayed women and girls favorably as intelligent, hardworking, decisive, courageous, and complete human beings—women who were in control of their own lives. It was a grueling undertaking, but she was determined to find inspirational stories for young women. In her relentless search, she uncovered stories from all around the world, from diverse and rich regions, such as sub-Saharan Africa. She assembled over one hundred folktales celebrating strong female heroines who were fearless, knowledgeable, fair, and wise, and gave the book its befitting title: *Fearless Girls, Wise Women and Beloved Sisters*.

In her search, she discovered that some stories have been changed over the years, presenting women as beautiful, pure, passive, and helpless victims to fit with the social mores demanded at those times. She found that in one of the earliest versions of "Little Red Riding Hood," for instance, the girl defeated the wolf all by herself in the forest; in another version, she defeated the wolf together with her grandmother, with no man involved.

Kathleen is a pioneer, trendsetter, and hero. She's done what women of change ought to do: find ways to counter the negative messages that constantly condition females to feel inferior and incomplete. In her book, she shares positive

---

9   Kathleen Ragan, *Fearless Girls, Wise Women and Beloved Sisters* (New York: W. W. Norton & Company, 2000), xxiii.

and inspiring stories of women as daring, courageous, determined, and assertive.

In the story "Davit" from Georgia, a young girl named Svetlana embarks upon a fabulous quest to cure her brother's illness after doctors, wise men, magicians, and old women have failed. Svetlana decides to travel to the sun to ask for guidance. With dauntless persistence, she sets out on her journey wearing a pair of shoes made from stone. "Until these wear out, I will not give up on my journey to see the sun," Svetlana says.[10] She returns with a cure for her brother as well as solutions for the needy that she meets on her travels. This story not only portrays Svetlana as a courageous individual, but shows that fearlessness, decisiveness, determination, and an adventurous spirit are characteristics possessed by both sexes. The story subtly encourages women to be adventurous and to explore things and places that will broaden their horizons.

In "The Flying Head" from the Iroquois, a young mother takes a stand against a monster after her whole village goes into hiding. "Someone must make a stand against this monster. It might as well be me," she says.[11] This young mother realizes that she and her child might die. However, to save her village and all the other villages threatened by the Flying Head, she chooses to confront the monster. This choice demands more than spontaneous bravery—it requires courage, which she demonstrates. This story refutes the myth that women are incapable of taking care of themselves and need to be saved. The heroine takes her destiny into her own hands with quiet resolve, portraying women as assertive leaders and

---

10 Ragan, *Fearless Girls, Wise Women and Beloved Sisters*, 77.

11 Ragan, *Fearless Girls, Wise Women and Beloved Sisters*, 105.

fearless warriors.

In "I'm Tipingee, She's Tipingee, We're Tipingee, Too" from Haiti, "Tipingee and her large network of friends gaily present a united front against the old man and stepmother who would do Tipingee harm."[12] This story demonstrates how much woman and girls can accomplish when they work together. Regardless of age, education, financial means, or social standing, we can defeat even the biggest and strongest forces that oppose us. This story debunks the idea that girls are inherently envious and competitive with each other.

Kathleen realized that the absence of heroines in stories teaches girls that strong women don't exist or matter. The stories she put together not only show women as complete beings but also counter some of the most prominent negative themes prevalent in children and adult stories.

MESSAGES OF WOMEN'S WORTH IN CHILDREN'S STORIES

BEAUTY

The theme of beauty is present in many children's stories such as "Sleeping Beauty" and "Snow White," as well as many folk tales; beauty or attractiveness is portrayed as a woman's most important attribute. Beauty is often an indicator of a woman's chance of future happiness; the beautiful girls get their princes and live happily ever after. By presenting the heroines as flawless and perfect, stories insinuate that beauty is the most desirable quality in women and encourage women to strive to attain it. Additionally, youthful, physical beauty is seen as good while older women are presented as ugly and wicked.

---

12 Ragan, *Fearless Girls, Wise Women and Beloved Sisters*, 155.

This tells young girls that they should fight the aging process rigorously. However, older, evil men are rarely mentioned in these stories, which takes the pressure off of men worrying about their looks or their fading youthfulness. In some African cultures, more bride price is paid for girls who are considered more beautiful.

PURITY

The theme of purity is presented in most children's stories, and is only used to describe girls. The idea of purity as a desirable trait in women first surfaced in the eighteenth century with the myth of chastity belts serving as tokens of marital fidelity.[13] This notion continues to be promoted and encouraged by religious and cultural norms. Today in the United States,[14] purity balls are federally funded daddy-daughter dances that are organized by religious intuitions. At these dances, the young girls pledge their virginities to their fathers, who in turn pledge to be the caretakers of their daughters' virginities. In some instances, fathers give their daughters a lock-and-key necklace; the father keeps the key and hands it to his son-in-law on the wedding night. This tells young girls that their bodies first belong to their father and then their husband. It informs girls that their value is tied to their virginity and that they are no longer pure or valuable if they have sex outside of marriage. However, there aren't purity balls for boys.

In my high school, we had purity pledge cards with the

---

13 "The Secret Histories of Chastity Belts." Semmelweis Medical History Museum, Library and Archives of the History of Medicine. Budapest, Hungary. July 23–October 24, 2010. www.semmelweis. museum.hu/muzeum/kiallitasok/erenyov/reszletes_en.html

14 Anastasia Kousakis, "Why is America So Obsessed with Virginity?" *HuffPost*, May 8, 2009.

words "True love waits." We signed the cards, pledging our virginity to God until our wedding night. There were also cards for secondary virgins, those who had fallen astray; they could recommit their lives to God and wait until their wedding night to have sex. These cards created guilt and pressure—most girls signed the cards out of fear of being judged as bad girls who planned on having premarital sex, and the girls who signed the secondary virgin cards were automatically labeled as immoral. These practices tell girls that they are only valuable when they are virgins—their value diminishes once they have sex. All over the world, derogatory words such as "damaged goods" are used to describe pregnant women. In Cameroon, the pidgin word commonly used for pregnant women is *eketeh*, which typically describes a beat-up car, or a car that has been in an accident but is still being driven.

DOMESTICITY AND PASSIVITY

Besides beauty and purity, a woman must also be submissive in order to be successful. A beautiful woman is considered good when she is pure, submissive, and domesticated. She accepts her lot in life, does as she is told, and doesn't question gender norms and rules while she waits patiently for her prince to appear. Passivity, domesticity, purity, and beauty complement each other. A girl who is beautiful and pure but makes her own decisions is usually punished. This teaches girls that they'll be rewarded if they adhere to the gender roles. I remember a popular African folktale we were often told as children:

There was once a beautiful girl whose beauty was talked about in all the neighboring countries; people traveled great distances just to get a glimpse of her. Many suit-

ors traveled from afar to ask for her hand in marriage, but she turned them all down—even the ones everyone thought would be the best fit for her. Some were wealthy, strong, and good looking.

One day, a suitor arrived from a faraway land on an expensive carriage drawn by beautiful horses. He was tall, handsome, and dressed in a fancy suit. She immediately fell for him despite the protest from her parents and the community. The two were married and they left for the man's homeland. Soon after they stepped out of her village, bizarre things began to happen. A man approached them and said, "Give me back my carriage." Another man demanded the horses and the newlyweds continued on foot. In every town, it turned out that the suitor had borrowed an item to impress the girl and persuade her to marry him; none of the items (it turns out, not even his body parts) were his. They got to his house late at night and it was too dark to see clearly. Exhausted, she fell asleep and woke up the next morning on top of a grave. It turns out the man was a ghost who had come from the land of the dead just to teach her a lesson in humility and submissiveness. The girl spent the rest of her days crying under a tree and singing a sad song, calling on her parents to come and rescue her.

I was terrified by this story and had nightmares for many nights. I reminded myself often when I was younger to obey the rules so I wouldn't end up like this arrogant girl.

In February 2014, I attended a youth conference that cemented my belief that children's stories tie children's potentials to their gender's expectations and affect them as adults. During the breakout session, my group was assigned an enlightening activity with participants separated into groups of five. Each group was given certain items to study and was instructed to write down common themes and report the findings back to the main group.

My group got birthday cards for three- to five-year-old boys and girls. The cards for the girls were mostly pink, flowery, and brightly colored and said, "My little princess," "My little sunshine," and, the most amusing one, "Being cute gets you great stuff." The cards for the boys were mostly blue or had pictures of cars and said, "My little warrior," "Future doctor," and "Mommy's little hero," with other positive and empowering affirmations. A group next to us was given games for five- to seven-year-old children. The games for the girls involved learning how to bake cupcakes, dress up dolls, and play house or nurse, while the games for the boys involved trying to figure out difficult puzzles, fighting crimes, building things, and playing doctor.

When we got back to the larger group, we asked: Why aren't girls encouraged to learn how to build things? Why can't boys play house? Why are girls encouraged to become nurses but not doctors? Why aren't boys encouraged to learn how to cook? Why have parents and adults bought into this way of thinking? I mentioned that not all girls like pink and love to cook and not all boys love blue and like to build things. I added that a skill such as cooking should be taught to everyone, because it is a lifesaving skill that anyone can learn regardless of gender. I also pointed out that some of the top chefs in the world are men. Why it is okay for men to cook professionally but not to cook for themselves or their families? The participants were all shocked to realize that even children's toys are being used as conditioning tools to promote patriarchal principles.

A few men and women in the group posited that gender roles arose due to the need for control, a fear born out of changing times and roles. When women entered the workforce, men feared what would happen if they weren't the sole breadwinners, providers, and protectors. Men not only resisted the change, but they also devised gender norms and roles to maintain the status quo. Hence, duties typically done by women when they stayed home, such as cooking, were considered inferior "women's work," and men had to avoid these duties to maintain a false sense of superiority. We concluded our session by challenging ourselves to question every action we take when making decisions for ourselves, our spouses, and our children, to determine if the decisions are driven by gender norms. If we realize that the decisions are made solely to support these ideologies, they should be challenged.

While attending a conference on youth development, I sat across from a fascinating lady and listened to her share amazing stories on women's and girls' empowerment. She was not only aware of the effect of this damaging concept but had made it her life's mission to educate, advocate for, and mentor women and girls and to recognize their personal power. I got into a conversation with her and found out we were birds of a feather—she quickly became a role model. After being invited to participate at one of her annual events organized to empower young girls, I was blown away by her initiative, tenacity, dedication, and passion for girls.

WOMAN OF CHANGE

WOMAN OF CHANGE

DR. VERNA CORNELIA PRICE

Verna Cornelia Price, PhD, is a force to be reckoned with—an intelligent, driven, strong, and compassionate lady with a radiant smile to match her big heart. She walks with her head held high and exudes confidence. She is a two-time bestselling author, motivational speaker, executive coach, educator, and founder of Girls in Action, a nonprofit organization that focuses on empowering young girls. Additionally, she is a wife and a mother to four amazing children.

Born in Nassau, Bahamas, she grew up on the small Kent Island with her maternal grandmother, who instilled the concept of being whole and complete in all of her grandchildren by teaching them to do things for themselves. As children, their grandmother taught them about the value of education and hard work by sending them to school and giving them chores and responsibilities. The chores gave them guidance and discipline and made them feel accomplished.

By the tender age of five, Verna discovered her passion for teaching, so she started to teach other kids on the island how to read, write, and ride a bike—she owned the only bike on the island. Her grandmother encouraged and nurtured Verna's love for teaching, and she knew from that young age that teaching was her calling.

At age ten, Verna immigrated to the United States, which

was a challenging transition. Despite facing adversity and set-backs, she held onto her grandmother's words of wisdom encouraging her to never give up and to work hard. Verna continued to work diligently at school and excelled in her classes despite experiencing prejudice. She describes the second half of her childhood as horrible and the third half as an awakening. Today, as a leader, a visionary, and a woman of change, she strives to instill the concept of being whole and complete in women and girls.

In 2005, she created Girls in Action as a response to a cry for help from a local Minneapolis high school. The school administrator was heartbroken over girls who had lost their sense of self and were in dire need of positive female role models. At the school, Dr. Verna witnessed girls disrespecting themselves in various ways: getting in physical and verbal altercations, getting pregnant, and behaving destructively. As a woman of change, she saw something positive underneath their dysfunction—beautiful, intelligent, gifted young women who weren't living up to their full potentials. Dr. Verna immediately sprang into action, taking on the challenge to enable the girls to see their worth. She quickly designed a curriculum aimed to motivate, empower, and prepare the girls to succeed in life.

The very first time she met with the girls, she invited other women from the community to join her. The girls were instructed to stand in a circle, holding hands; the women formed a protective circle around the girls, creating a barrier of love. The ladies took turns giving positive, encouraging words to the girls:

"We're your mothers; we're here for you."

"You can call on us and lean on us."

"You never have to walk alone."

"You are worthy and valuable."

Positive changes were noticeable by the end of the program's first year. The girls developed respect for themselves and others, believing in themselves and catching up with their school work. Today, the program serves over five hundred girls yearly across thirteen different school districts and five community sites. Dr. Verna explains why she agreed to take on this challenge: "Empowering girls is a must—it's the only way forward for any community. Community is centered on women—as the women go, so does the community. Women are incredible, powerful, and influential people God has created as anchors in the world. "

She acknowledges that it's difficult for women to make potential impacts in the world when they're taught that they are inferior, marginalized, disenfranchised, and discriminated against. Women of change must stand up, empower, and instill a sense of self and wholeness in disenfranchised women and girls while providing opportunities for the future.

In her personal life, Dr. Verna's mantra is "There is more than enough," and she explains that a lot of women are taught to operate with a scarcity philosophy that creates fear and unhealthy competition. She believes that there are more than enough resources in the world for each of us to fulfill our destinies. One person getting ahead in life doesn't prevent another person from achieving his or her goals. Dr. Verna calls on every woman to operate with a more-than-enough philosophy, to take comparisons and competition out of her daily practice, and to do what she has to do for herself and others without self-neglect.

Dr. Verna's goal is to extend the Girls in Action ideology and program to many different communities around the world; she aims to create positive female representations in every community and to foster the concept of women as whole and complete beings. In January 2016, Girls in Action expanded to Kenya, and launched its first African chapter in partnership with Light of Hope.

It's crucial for women to feel complete and whole, because it's our personal responsibility to take care of ourselves—to bring and feel joy and fulfillment in our lives before we can be of service to others. Feeling incomplete robs women of becoming their authentic selves, because their main focus is finding someone else to complete them. This feeling of incompleteness creates doubt, insecurity, emptiness, unhealthy comparison, and competition. It's essential to raise girls and boys as equals so the world can benefit from each person's unique abilities. Dr. Verna showed us examples of how women of change can fight this existing culture and enable other women and girls to know that they matter.

TAKEAWAYS

- You are worthy, valuable, and a complete being. Your worth isn't determined by your beauty, purity, domestication, submissiveness, or marital status. Your worth never decreases.

- Don't become a reflection of the negative words used against you.

- Marriage is not an achievement—there is no certificate of completion. If you choose to get married, only marry a partner who honors and respects you. An achievement is defined as the successful completion of a task usually requiring special skills or ability.

- Fight patriarchal norms and encourage girls to view themselves as whole by writing stories with positive female protagonists, or support projects that promote those ideologies.

DISCUSSION QUESTIONS

- Where did you get most of your ideas and beliefs regarding your gender and its role in marriage? Were these ideas modeled for you? Can you remember any stories that shaped your ideas and notions about marriage? Did these stories and ideas empower you? Did they distort your self-image and make you feel powerless and incomplete? What did these stories do for you? What can you do to ensure there are more stories with positive female protagonists for young girls?

- Can you remember a book you read or a movie you watched that had a positive female protagonist? How did that impact you? What can you do to ensure that there are more female role models for younger girls? What can you do to become a role model for younger girls?

- What are your most positive attributes? If you can't think of them, ask the three closest women in your life to list your five most positive attributes and do the same for them. Keep your list of attributes in a visible place so you can see them every day.

- Give an example of a patriarchal norm or expectation that had a great impact in your life and made you feel incomplete. What steps did you use to overcome that lie? Share with a friend.

KEY WORDS

Whole

Self-respect

Awakening

Complete

Personal power

Potential

Authentic self

Personal mantra

Protagonist

Worth

Economic success

Beauty

Value

Forgiveness

CHAPTER FOUR

ENGAGING MEN AND WOMEN AS ALLIES

We cannot all succeed
when half of us are held back.
—Malala Yousafzai

I didn't experience gender discrimination while growing up, because my grandparents (Mom and Dad) provided equal opportunities for their children and grandchildren. My grandfather was a man of change and ahead of his time in many ways: he truly believed that humans were equal, each with their own unique abilities, and that men weren't superior to women. He didn't favor his sons over his daughters or disrespect his wife; they made decisions together. When Mom and Dad handed out pocket allowances, the boys and girls received the same amount. Dad was also a meticulous man of few words and a strict disciplinarian. The only times he excitedly called us by our nicknames was when we excelled in school. He expected all of his children and grandchildren to attain a higher education and spoke about its importance repeatedly. I remember a remark he made when I was about nine. I was reading a book, an activity he enjoyed seeing us do. He turned to me and said, "Iya Maks, to consider yourself educated you have to get at least a master's degree. Never stop reading and learning. You will become more knowledgeable and broaden your reasoning and thinking faculties."

Getting approval and encouragement from my grandfather, one of the most intelligent people I knew, was exhilarating. I had a lot of respect for him and developed more respect when I learned how he stood by his principles and didn't buckle under societal pressures.

When Mom and Dad made the decision to send their children (including their daughters) to college, not every community member agreed. Dad faced a lot of opposition and criticism from his friends and other men in the community who felt that he had gone too far with his ideas on equality. They accused him of creating a new set of problems for the community. By sending his daughters to college, they said he was telling them that they were equals with men. The higher education would fill his daughters' heads with delusions of grandeur; they would be self-sufficient, not need men, and wouldn't be submissive if they got married.

The community feared that Dad's ideologies and examples could become common practice, disrupting the normal order of things. A primary education was more than good enough for a girl; girls were created to be wives and mothers who took care of the home, not breadwinners. They didn't need a college education to cook or take care of babies. Besides, girls weren't as smart as boys; sending them to college would be a waste of money. Dad told his critics, "Girls have brains just as boys. Why not let them use their brains to the best of their abilities? Girls getting an education doesn't prevent boys from getting educated; it only improves the community. I will provide an education for all my kids and raise them the way I see fit."

Years later, when Dad threw college graduation parties for

his daughters, those same men who had opposed him gave him firm handshakes and congratulated him for his children's achievements. I remember when my mother became a journalist—as a man of change, Dad seized that opportunity to again educate his friends about the importance of educating girls. On the nights my mother read the seven-thirty English news, Dad would invite his friends over to watch with him, because they didn't have television sets in their homes. Even though he didn't drink alcohol, Dad provided beer and put his friends at ease. Once my mom popped on the screen, they would scream in delight. "Look at our daughter!" Dad would then say proudly, with a grin of satisfaction on his face:

"That is Ndinge, my first daughter; she is a journalist. The second, Beatrice, is a magistrate and will become a judge in a few years. Inez teaches English and French in a high school in Limbe. Sandra is in Saker, one of the best girls' secondary schools in the country. She will attend the university next year. You see this television set right here? My daughter Beatrice bought it for us. See what girls can accomplish; my daughters are smart and educated."

His friends looked at him in awe. I bet they were thinking that they, too, should have sent their daughters to college rather than into marriages right after primary school.

Even though I was raised in a home where both parents were equal partners, I was quite aware that men and women were not equal in Cameroon and in the world at large—it was all around me in the community. Young girls had to return home to cook immediately after school while their brothers stayed back and played sports. Some girls were pulled out of school when finances were tight in favor of their brothers' educations, and others were married off even though they wanted to stay in school. Women who worked nine-to-five jobs (just like their husbands) still returned home and headed straight for the kitchen without a moment's rest. Even if their husbands stayed home all day, the women still had to do the cooking, because it's considered taboo for men to cook.

Mom had been a teacher (and thus knew the value of education) and would have ensured that all her children got an education even if Dad wasn't supportive. However, as I reflect on my upbringing, I realize that the process would have been much more difficult and stressful for both Mom and her daughters if Dad hadn't believed in equality. My mother, aunties, and I probably wouldn't have turned out as well as we have. Knowing we had support from both parents (and grandparents) was an extra boost and motivated us to work harder. Dad's involvement and concern for our well-being and education made us understand how valuable, smart, and worthy we are. We didn't see ourselves as lesser humans thanks to the equality at home, though we each occasionally struggled with the ideas and expectations of our gender due to societal norms. The pressures and conditioning would've gotten the best of us if our roots were not well-established at home. We had the approval of, and were held in high esteem by, the most important man in our lives.

After noticing a few of Dad's peers change their minds and attitudes towards girls' education through his conversations with them, and using his daughters as examples to emphasize his points, I now believe in the power of effective dialoguing. Conversations can make men and women allies—even women who are still on the sidelines about joining or supporting the women's empowerment movement. I wholeheartedly agree with people who are aware that the only way to get gender equality, stop women's marginalization, and grow the economy is for men and women to work together. We all need to be educated and effectively communicate that we all win when we elevate one another and work together.

The art of dialoguing has proven to be one of the most effective ways for women and men to become allies—so much so that organizations such as Stichting Nederlandse Vrijwilligers (SNV, "Foundation of Netherlands Volunteers," Netherlands Development Organization), which has branches around the world (including the United States), has crafted an effective dialogue model. This model lets men and women have in-depth conversations that allow men to see the real value of women and realize how all humans benefit when they work together. The SNV creates dialogues using a "Balancing Benefit approach"[15] and has recorded amazing results by introducing household dialogues and showing couples the benefits of working as a team in countries where patriarchal influences are strongly felt.

In these situations, the dialogue focuses on how the whole family benefits when spouses work together. The dialogue challenges social norms that hold women back from achieving their full potentials; it shows how the community is worsened by not allowing women to utilize their skills.

Personally, I can attest to the incredible power of dialoguing and presenting information aimed to educate and inform, not to scold or point accusatory fingers. In 2014, I gave a presentation in honor of International Women's Day and invited men to attend. A few men were apprehensive about the talk—one in particular was adamant about not attending the event, saying, "Ms. LaBelle, you know I have a lot of respect for you

---

15 Sarah de Smet, "The power of dialogue in accelerating gender equality," What's new? (blog), SNV, February 2017, www.snv.org/update/power-dialogue-accelerating-gender-equality.

and my daughter looks up to you, but on this issue I'll pass. Women's empowerment is all about women's desire to control men and to become the leaders. You women already have everything. What else do you want?"

I assured him that women's empowerment is not about women being in control of men, but is actually about women being in control of their own lives. It's about women's rights to be respected, treated with fairness, and given access to education and resources within their communities—to be allowed freedom to design their own futures and be full, contributing members of society. I promised that he would be enlightened by the presentation. He relented and showed up at the event.

During the presentation, I shared the story of Dad's influence on our lives and how much it enabled us to become who we are today. I then talked about my visit with the girls at the Teenage Mothers' Institute in Buea, Cameroon. I asked the audience to imagine how much better the community of Buea would be if those girls were given the opportunity to become what they desired. Lastly, I shared stories of real women who were marginalized yet became financially stable, provided education for their children, and changed the dynamics of their families and communities once they were provided educational opportunities, loans, and other resources. I concluded the presentation by challenging everyone in the audience to become an ally, starting within their families, places of work and worship, and communities, and added that we all have the power to make positive changes in the world. After the presentation, the man walked up to me and said:

"Ms. LaBelle, thank you so much for an amazing and eye-opening presentation. I'm a man, an African man at that. I was raised to believe men are in charge of women and make the decisions and rules. I didn't realize that a lot of our cultural and religious practices hold women back. The points you made are valid, but these aren't things men think about. I guess it's because we are the beneficiaries of this system. We don't realize that we also suffer when we put all these restrictions on women. I'm a father of a girl and I wouldn't want to interfere negatively with her journey. Now I know that women's empowerment is about equality and all humans working together. Thank you for the presentation. I promise you I will do better—we will do better."

While working on this project, it dawned on me that the best way to make allies out of men would be to talk to real men who have already joined the struggle: men who are pro-feminists, fight against gender inequality, and have the foresight to realize that we all suffer when women are marginalized. Their insights would enable those still on the fence about gender equality to see the wisdom in us all working together. I knew that there are men in the United States who identify as pro-feminist and speak openly about gender issues; I wondered if I could find such men in Africa. As fate would have it, while browsing online, I came across a brilliant and honest write-up by an African man, Victor Ibeh, living in Africa—it was about some of the underlying causes of divorce in today's society. I was intrigued and contacted him. The piece contained some of the facts that today's women have been singing to deaf ears. To see those same facts pointed out by a man made me do a little dance. Victor writes,

> *The rate of divorce is increasing daily, not because marriages of the past were better than marriages today, but because the key actors in marital longevity of the previous generation are no longer willing to put up with insanity. Most marriages in the past lasted for so long*

because women back then were taught and compelled to accept their subservient roles and to endure everything that came with their marriages.

However, the twenty-first century woman is on a journey of self-discovery, reorientation, and fulfillment. She is learning daily to build her self-esteem and to put her personal happiness above matrimonial longevity. This doesn't mean that these women are unwilling to work towards a long-lasting marriage. It simply means they are not willing to sacrifice their eternal peace and sanity simply to make a marriage long-lasting.

Strangely enough, some people are pointing accusing fingers at women, claiming they are responsible for failing marriages. The truth is, some men are unwilling to contribute their personal quota and continue to hold on to the old belief that it is a woman who makes the marriage work. This ideology is gradually losing its hold on women. Women are now living with the mindset that for a marriage to work there should be 100 percent contribution from both parties.

This is not the time to point accusing fingers at women; it is time to work together as equal partners. If you want your marriage to last, work on it as though your life depended on it; this work cannot be done by one person. Both parties must be committed to it. Make no mistake about it; if you insist on not treating your partner well, you will lose her/him. Marriage is no longer a death sentence.

It is stupid and arrogant for anyone to risk getting a divorce because they insist on not treating their partner with respect and dignity.[16]

---

16 Victor Ibeh's Facebook page. Accessed September 28, 2016. https://www.facebook.com/victor.c.ibeh.

MAN OF CHANGE

VICTOR IBEH

Victor Ibeh has always been a feminist at heart. As a young boy growing up in Nigeria, he spoke out when girls were harassed, treated unfairly, or discriminated against. In 2010, he discovered that there was a name given to his ideology: feminism. After learning about feminism, he decided to help educate the masses on the importance and benefits of empowering women and girls.

As he got deeper into learning about feminism, he saw an upsurge in toxic masculinity within his community—men acting in vile and repugnant ways, controlling women's lives under the guise of tradition and religion. After identifying culture and religion as the two main factors used to marginalize and oppress women within Nigeria, he created a nonprofit organization, VILVAR, to promote feminism on a larger scale and to enable women to realize just how important they are to the overall success of their communities. "There is so much we can't achieve until women are given the opportunity to unleash the power within them."

Both men and women have accused him of fighting against tradition and customs and promoting ideologies that they claim aren't African. He counters these accusations by pointing out certain archaic traditions that men are moving away from: In certain tribes, men were expected to wrestle with the village wrestling champion to show agility and prove that they were responsible and ready for marriage. In other tribes, men were expected to build two houses (one in the village and another in the city) to show that they were responsible before getting married. Certain tribes practice tribal circumcision, which was done without anesthesia by tribal leaders on grown men to show strength, the crossing-over into manhood, and readiness to deal with adult responsibilities. Victor then accuses the men of practicing cultural selective observation, holding onto practices that benefit them. To the women who critique his work, Victor acknowledges that their attacks are based on years of conditioning; he hopes to educate them through dialogue.

To his critics who have cited biblical scriptures to support male superiority, basing their claim on the idea that woman was created from man to be his helper, Victor (who is also a preacher) uses the Bible to debunk the myth. He bases his foundation of feminism on the Bible by citing passages which state that God created men and women equal. He further points to several passages in the Bible where God is referred to as a "helper." He then dumbfounds his critics by asking, "When you pray and refer to God as 'my helper,' does this mean then that you believe you're superior to God?"

Victor believes that more men will join the pro-feminist movement with more dialogue and education on the topic. He has witnessed positive changes in some of the men he has counseled; a few have publicly declared that this new perspective has improved their families' lives. Victor believes men should be part of women's empowerment because women's empowerment is human empowerment.

As I continued reading about men who described themselves as pro-feminists, I came across the profile of Rob Okun, an American, and was fascinated by his dedication and length of service in the movement.

MAN OF CHANGE

ROB OKUN

Rob is a writer, speaker on gender justice, editor, activist, and psychotherapist whose pro-feminist involvement spans three decades. He learned about the concept of feminism at home: he grew up in a loving, peaceful home where respect and equality were not only words—they were demonstrated. He describes his father as gentle and his mother as strong and calls them his role models.

Nonetheless, Rob came of age in the 1950s and '60s and was influenced by the bias of male superiority as a young man. However, when he became a parent, he and his wife made a conscious effort to raise their children as equals. After their first child, a girl, they waited three years before having their second child, a boy. They were glad that their firstborn was female, as living with strong, empowered girls allows boys to grow up with a palpable example of equality in their family, counteracting social messages suggesting that men should be dominant.

Rob realized that one way to fight patriarchy and promote gender equality was to redefine manhood. While working at a men's center, including leading intervention groups for abusive men, he decided to report on the center's work—promoting a new vision of manhood without violence, as well as equality and fairness between the sexes. He combined his careers in journalism and men's work to tell the men's stories. To fully participate in the movement, he challenged himself to become comfortable with sharing his inner life and vulnerabilities with others, which he describes as the key to overcoming challenges and fears. He encouraged the men at the shelter to examine ways that they could contribute to the movement to achieve a gender-just world. He explains,

"Men have a real opportunity to examine the privileges we receive for no other reason than that we arrived on the planet in male-identified bodies. Once we seriously consider our sense of entitlement, the conditions have been cultivated to have an awakening and to join with women in working for gender justice."

The knowledge that he is not the only man in the pro-feminist movement has been a huge component of why he has developed and maintained the attitude of "keep on keeping on," despite the backlash and disapproval from other men. In his three decades as a feminist, he has witnessed the number of collaborative men's and women's organizations growing larger:

"That sense of growing a movement, and feeling it strengthen, is a tremendously satisfying counterbalance to those who criticize, who suggest men doing this work are 'gender traitors.'"

Rob quickly recognized that, despite the growth of the movement over the decades, pro-feminist men were still under the radar; their work wasn't being reported significantly. This created a false notion that there were few to no men involved in the fight for gender equality. His advice to any young person who wants to start a pro-feminist movement is to find one person who agrees with you—this one person will remind you that you aren't alone. Then, begin with your highest vision of what is possible and put that vision out to others. He asserts, "You'll be surprised—and elated—to discover how many people will be drawn to your light." Rob continues advocating for the social transformation of masculinity by serving as a featured speaker at colleges and universities, cochair of the Men's Resource Center for Change's board of directors, and a steering committee member of the Center for the Study of Men and Masculinities.

After interviewing Rob, I purchased his book, *Voice Male: The Untold Story of the Pro-Feminist Men's Movement*, to learn more about the pro-feminism movement. While reading through the stories, I came across the profile of Gilbert Salazar. His involvement in the movement was intriguing and unique from all the others'. I reached out to Gilbert and discovered that he has a real passion for equality and wants to help young men break free from the chains of masculinity.

GILBERT SALAZAR

Gilbert is a young Chicano man born and raised in Santa Ana, California. He is a theater educator, artist, restorative justice practitioner, writer, and circle keeper. As the oldest of three children and the oldest of sixteen grandchildren, Gilbert believes he has a responsibility to lead young people by positive example. Gilbert and his siblings spent their early years with their mother at their maternal grandparents' house away from their dominating father. He describes these years as "joyful, full of games and laughter."

When the children eventually lived with both parents, their home was no longer loving and peaceful. Gilbert was not taught about fairness or about considering men and women equals. His father, who was a macho Latino man, demanded to be respected and feared above all else. Gilbert's mother, however, was taught to cater to the children's needs first, such as by serving their meals before any adults' meals. This always created conflict between Gilbert's parents. There was constant unrest at home, usually stemming from economic hardship, which caused his father to take out his frustration on the family. Gilbert's father didn't have a permanent job, but was taught to value his masculinity and the role of provider and breadwinner. As a construction worker, he couldn't work in poor weather or during an economic downturn. He felt like less of a man when his role as breadwinner was threatened and he couldn't meet his financial responsibilities. In turn, he became violent and abusive, both psychologically and emotionally.

Gilbert's father also used corporal punishment as a form of discipline, especially when his orders weren't followed. Gilbert admits that the physical abuse was bad, but the scars he got were actually from emotional and psychological trauma. Every time his mother stepped in during a physical fight to protect him from his father, Gilbert's father would become spiteful and demeaning: "Your balls ain't big enough to step up to me, boy. You hide under your mother's skirt like a little bitch," he said, insinuating that Gilbert wasn't man enough—weak, incapable of taking care of himself, and needing his mother's protection. Those words were damaging and made Gilbert question his developing masculinity. The more he internalized the words, the more he became confused and started to question, "Am I male enough? How male do I want to be when what's in front of me is damaging? What's my identity outside of my mother and home? Who am I?"

As he matured, he realized that the best way for parents to fight gender inequality and violence is to raise their children as equals and to mirror equality and respect in the way they treat one another. It's important for parents to teach their children that no one person's role in the family is more important than another's. Based on his upbringing, Gilbert strongly felt that he needed to work with young boys in his community to teach them about the other aspects of masculinity.

After completing his undergrad studies and a service-learning project on youth development, violence, and gang affiliations, he landed a job as a prevention educator at a sexual violence prevention center. He was first trained in how to become a crisis counselor. This training forced him to dig deeper into himself and to recognize that, as a man, his voice was needed in the fight against the oppression and sexual assault of women. He realized during his training that the best way to help would be to prevent rapes and assaults from happening. This realization made him more determined to start his work with boys to teach them to take responsibility for their actions, avoid using violence, and treat women with respect. In turn, this could prevent thousands of women from experiencing violence and trauma. He asserts that, if rape is prevented, there will be no need for rape crisis counseling. It's an effective upstream approach to rape that Gilbert wholeheartedly believes in: preventing something horrible from happening rather than providing treatment after the incident occurs. He hopes that more resources can be directed toward prevention education and training.

Working with teenage boys revealed that much younger children are taught to tie their masculinity to violence. As a response, Gilbert started facilitating two MyStrength clubs that focus on preventing young men from committing sexual violence for the first time.

Gilbert realized that some young men are attracted to violence because they're taught that it signifies masculinity. Therefore, the best way to counter this would be having strong, selfless, and courageous men become mentors and role models to teach young men about self-respect, respect for women, other aspects of masculinity, and the fact that actions have consequences. Gilbert also realized that most young men are opposed to violence, want healthy relationships, and are willing to work hard to achieve their goals but don't know how to actually do this. The boys in his MyStrength clubs were willing participants, showing that young men can be turned around and won't become perpetrators with the right influences in their lives.

Men and women have to educate each other about the effects of violence on families and communities. The anti-violence work isn't progressing as quickly as it could, since mostly women are engaged in this work while the majority of the perpetrators are men. Gilbert calls on more men to quickly become part of this movement, for both women's and men's liberation. Men are also victims of masculinity's stereotypes, though not to the extent of women. Men need to understand the consequences and limitations of patriarchy and their role in it in order to become unshackled. Gilbert also believes it will make more of an impact on men if they're educated by an enlightened man rather than a woman, so it isn't perceived as a battle of the sexes. He further challenges men who are aware of and honest about the privilege they enjoy to become educators.

Gilbert believes in creating conversation topics about anti-violence and feminism that allow women and men to work side by side without one gender vilifying the other. He struggled to appear small or less threatening to put his female colleagues at ease, especially since in the past a few complained that they were uncomfortable with his presence without explaining why. He later discovered that this is a problem faced by other men of color who work with women in the anti-violence movement; the men feel unwelcome by their female colleagues. This suspicious attitude discourages well-intentioned men.

Gilbert's main focus, besides restorative justice work, is creating a full stage production of a play he wrote about violence and masculinity, including workshops with audience members. He is weaving together stories of young boys and men he worked with over the years in hopes of sparking a conversation among the audience members, challenging them to see the masks that we all wear. Gilbert hopes that we can become accountable for healing when we learn how we harm others with our actions.

These highlighted men of change demonstrate the power of men dialoguing with each other and the difference it makes in the world when men and women are allies. We need more men to recognize the importance of collaboration and equality and to join the pro-feminist movement. To become an ally is to realize that both genders complement one another and that each person's skills are indispensable and should be respected and honored. It's about a shift in our mentality—to recognize that women's rights are human rights, and that women's liberation also liberates men. It's about collaboration between the sexes, not domination by one sex.

TAKEAWAYS

- Effective dialogues have the potential to educate, create an awakening, and bring about change.

- Fighting for gender equality and being part of the anti-violence movement are causes we can each positively contribute to, regardless of our upbringing.

- To achieve more effective and efficient results in the anti-violence and feminism movements, both men and women have to work alongside each other.

- Younger men need positive, strong role models; older men need to teach and demonstrate what masculinity is and guide young men along their journeys.

- Feminism benefits both genders (and the community as a whole), because it calls for fairness and equality for all humans.

DISCUSSION QUESTIONS

- Write down three ways that you can join or support the anti-violence and/or feminism movement(s). Share with the group.

- What steps can you take to create an anti-violence and/or feminism movement at your place of work, school, or worship? Share with the group.

- What steps can you take to create an effective dialogue about women's violence within your community? Share with the group.

- What are some ways you can become a role model to young men and women? Share with a friend.

- Besides volunteering or working at a battered women's shelter or crisis center, how else can you get in-depth knowledge about the damaging effects of violence on women, children, and the community as a whole? Share with the group.

KEY WORDS

Feminism

Collaboration

Anti-violence

Role models

Allies

Privilege

Dialogue

Advocate

Education

Ideology

Masculinity

Prevention

Social norms

Education

Upstream approach

CHAPTER FIVE

RAPE AND ABUSE— THE INCREDIBLE POWER OF RESILIENCE, FORGIVENESS, AND SELF-LOVE

A successful man (woman) is one who can lay a firm foundation with the bricks others have thrown at him (her).
—David Brinkley

Growing up, I knew that I was asking to be assaulted if I wore tight or short clothing. If I sat in a group of boys and something bad happened, I'd asked for it. I hardly ever heard about a man sent to prison for rape. Occasionally, a man was beaten for raping a woman (usually by her male relatives), but it was difficult to know if the rapist was beaten because he had hurt and violated a woman; the focus was typically on the shame brought upon the woman's family, because no man would marry a woman who had been touched outside of marriage. It's standard for the rapist to pay a fine to the woman's male relatives. The men from both the victim's and the rapist's families share drinks together at the end of their deliberations to show that they have buried the hatchet.

The victim is chastised and often told not to express her

emotions for fear that everyone in the community will be aware of her shame. In some cases, fathers throw their daughters out of their homes for tainting the family name, or the girls are forced to marry their rapists. In other cases, girls are sent to relatives far away with the hope that no one in their new surroundings will discover the dishonor they brought upon themselves—that they still stand a chance of getting married.

Generally, men and women blame the victims for the rape: "What was she doing over at his place—doesn't she know what a man wants when he invites a woman over?" or, "Why was she wearing such tight clothing—doesn't she know men are weak and easily tempted?" No one rebukes men for forcing themselves on women; instead, the victims are further victimized. Occasionally, lawmakers create more rules to control women and place the blame on the victims by pretending that the regulations are to protect women, saving them from themselves.

I remember a time back in the city of Kumba, Cameroon, when the mayor passed a law prohibiting girls from wearing short and tight clothing. He released policemen all over the city, granting them the authority to discipline and even detain girls who disobeyed the rules. Girls were literally chased through the market square and streets while being whipped with bamboo canes as onlookers laughed in delight, "Ei sweet. Who tell ei say make ei wear that kind short clothes? These girls dem over like for tempt man pikin." ("Serve her right. Who told her to wear such tight clothing? These girls love to tempt men.") During those times, assault rates increased. To my dismay, I found out that this practice was common all over Cameroon, as well as in other African countries, the Middle East, and Asia.

DR. EDWIGE MUBONZI

Dr. Edwige Mubonzi is a phenomenal woman, a true force of nature with a big personality. While interviewing her, I was reminded of Queen Yaa Asantewaa of the Ashanti tribe, who was a brave and intelligent fighter and led an army against the British Colonial Forces in the 1900s. Dr. Edwige is tall, beautiful, intelligent, fearless, and selfless, with a heart as big and rich as the minerals found in her native country of Congo. She has the courage of David and is determined to take down the Goliath destroying and ravaging her beautiful country: the endless war on minerals and the lack of women's rights.

Born to loving and supportive parents who are not only financially successful but also generous, she and her eight siblings were taught the importance of giving to others and standing up for what is right, using the biblical principle, "To whom much is given, much is required."

In 1998, when Edwige was just fourteen, her family was forced to abandon their home in Bukavu—they fled to the beautiful Idjwi Island for safety. A war had started in the east after Laurent-Désiré Kabila, a revolutionary backed by the Rwandan and Ugandan armies, invaded the Congo in 1997 and overthrew President Mobutu Sese Seko, who had been in power for thirty-two years. A year later, Kabila turned on his former backers and allowed the Hutu army—a group that had been dismantled after being accused of war crimes during the first Congo war of 1997—to regroup in the east. This resulted in a Rwandan-Ugandan joint invasion in 1998.

While on the island, Edwige immediately noticed that the

children were different from city children; they had big, puffy, swollen stomachs and cheeks. She remarked innocently to her father that the children in the village ate too much and was shocked and dismayed to learn that the children were actually suffering from malnutrition. She also encountered a pregnant woman about to give birth, but instead of joy there was terror, sadness, and whispers of the woman's impending death. Edwige was bewildered and asked why a pregnant woman was expected to die. She then learned that there were no doctors or midwives available, and that most women died during childbirth. The maternal and infant mortality rate was one of the highest in the world: 693 per 100,000 live births.[17] At that moment, she boldly and confidently declared to her father,

"I want to become a doctor when I'm older. I want to come back and build a hospital so pregnancy will become a joy. It isn't right and shouldn't be acceptable for a woman to die while bringing life into the world."

Her father was overjoyed and, being the ever-encouraging and supportive parent, purchased a piece of land for her.

"You are my daughter and I know you will do as you've said. Here is the land for you to build the hospital when you're ready."

During Edwige's final year in high school in 2004, her family had to flee from their home for a second time—this time to a UN refugee camp, since unrest had intensified in the east. The militia was reportedly going from house to house

---

17 "Maternal mortality ratio (modeled estimate, per 100,000 live births)," WHO, UNICEF, UNFPA, World Bank Group, and the United Nationals Population Division. Trends in Maternal Mortality: 1990 to 2015. Geneva, World Health Organization, 2015. data.worldbank.org/indicator/SH.STA.MMRT.

raping women and girls in the villages and cities. At the refugee camp, Edwige met many women who had been brutally raped, maimed, and violated. Her zeal to become a doctor became an even bigger priority at that moment.

The idea of becoming a doctor didn't resonate well with everyone in her community. Most people tried to discourage her, stating that being a doctor was a man's profession; they encouraged her to become a nurse or a domestic science teacher instead. Others tried talking her into getting married and starting a family like most girls in her community did after high school. Women and girls mounted more pressure on her as they sang songs mocking her marital status whenever she walked by. They called her *nyanya*, which means grandmother, a derogatory term they use for unmarried girls above high school age.

At medical school, Edwige faced adversity and alienation from male students and professors. She was one of three female students out of a class of eighty-two, and the school was like a boy's club. During lectures, the professors asked the female students outright, "Do you give up now?" which would evoke laughter and jeers from the male students. Every time Edwige got overwhelmed and felt like giving up, the images of the women and children on the island and in the refugee camp served as her driving force.

Right after graduating from medical school in 2011, she got two job offers and accepted both. The first position was to teach at her former university. As a woman of change, she took that position to serve as an inspiration to female medical students. The second position was to work as a general physician at Panzi Hospital in Bukavu. She volunteered at the Panzi mobile clinic in the ob-gyn department and learned how to perform specialty surgeries.

One of her duties at the mobile clinic was to travel to scattered villages that had been severely affected by the war, gathering rape victims and bringing them back to the clinic for surgery. In some cases, the rapists had left objects, such as a piece of wood or small knives, in the women's vaginas or inserted a pistol and fired into the woman. Dr. Edwige had to perform reconstructive surgeries, as most of the women suffered from the worst cases of traumatic fistula. Oftentimes, the women were raped in front of their husbands and children, causing irreparable psychological trauma for the whole family. The women were often shunned, alienated by their families and communities, and abandoned as though contagious. Rape was being used as an instrument of war so the militia could gain complete control over the country's minerals, especially coltan, of which the Congo alone produces 80 percent of the world's supply. With the support and funding from foreign companies greedily wanting coltan to produce cellphones, iPads, and laptops, the militia knew that if the women in a community were destroyed, the community would go to ruin.

Dr. Edwige was one of two women who worked in the mobile clinic, and they were often targeted. During one of their rescue missions to a village, her friend and coworker was kidnapped and found three days later. She had been raped repeatedly with objects by multiple men and was given drugs that left her confused and disoriented. Dr. Edwige was traumatized and knew that she was the next target. Regardless of the threats against her and the clinic staff, the work was of the utmost importance and had to continue. She stayed out of sight and didn't go into the field for two weeks, as was advised, but was eventually compelled to get back to work, because the rape victims wouldn't get into the clinic van to be driven back to the clinic without a female staff member present. They demanded Dr. Edwige by name and also requested that she perform their reconstructive surgeries. On her last field mission, there were 123 women raped in two villages. The outrageous number of women raped made the Democratic Republic of the Congo known as the "rape capital of the world," a term Dr. Edwige and other Congolese found offensive since their country is known for much more than rapes—abundant minerals, rich and diverse culture, beautiful music and language, and much more.

One day, while Dr. Edwige worked at the clinic, a rape survivor that Dr. Edwige had performed surgery on a year prior walked in with a baby in her arms. The baby, a six-month-old who was the result of the rape, had also been raped. Dr. Edwige was enraged and inconsolable. After performing a successful surgery on the baby, she started to advocate by calling for an end to the rapes, the trade of conflict minerals, and war. She wanted to educate the masses about the true nature of the war and who was actually benefiting from it. As a woman of change, she realized that it defeated the purpose of performing daily surgeries to do so while women and girls were still being raped, and she felt like an accomplice by not doing more. Unfortunately, her advocacy gained attention from the wrong set of people. One day, a man walked into the clinic and told Dr. Edwige that he was going to kill her, then left abruptly. Her boss, Dr. Denis Mukwege, who had survived a shooting, advised her to leave the country immediately. Dr. Edwige resisted the idea but figured she would be of no use to her people if dead.

With help from the UN, she arrived in Minnesota after three months of hiding under sheets while being driven to work. The only English words she knew upon her arrival were "yes" and "no." She was tempted to go back home after months of living alone in a hotel and fell ill. However, when she remembered how disgruntled and dejected her patients were, and how their lives changed after their surgeries, she realized that giving up was not an option. She remarked, "If those women, who have been violated in every way humanly possible, could still smile and be hopeful, then anyone can overcome tribulations."

Dr. Edwige believes in the strength of women and calls on women of change to stand up and speak out against rape and to work with rape victims. She states that women are the backbone of every economy and attests to how communities in the Congo that had been destroyed and devastated by women's rapes came back to life after the women were treated and regained their health and strength.

Currently, Dr. Edwige works a few hours per week and studies six hours daily for her boards. Her goal is to become a certified ob-gyn and to gather as much knowledge and expertise as she can before returning to the Congo, where she is most needed. In the Congo, she will be one of a few ob-gyns to attend to thousands of women. She continues on with her advocacy and has been invited twice to address the Minnesota state senate. During her speeches, she gave a history of the effects of war in the Congo and the rapes of thousands of women, and called for peaceful resolutions and an end to trading conflict minerals. Her passion for abused women, her courage, and her level of dedication and resilience show that she will definitely build that hospital on the land her father gave her. The people of Idjwi will have a hospital built by their own daughter, Dr. Edwige Mubonzi.

I was in awe as I listened to Dr. Edwige speak so passionately about an unmentionable subject, as well as the zeal with which she stands up for women's rights. To see an African woman speak so openly about a taboo subject while in the continent was mind blowing; she commanded my respect and gave me hope for the future.

I couldn't help but see the similarities of how rape and sexual assault victims are treated in both of our cultures; how frequently abuse and violence against women occurs and how swiftly it's swept under the rug; how violence toward women is normalized and the women are blamed for their abuse. The stigmatization of rape victims unfortunately doesn't only happen in Cameroon and the Congo; it's a worldwide problem. However, countries like the United States, the United Kingdom, and Canada, for example, have done a better job of protecting women and bringing perpetrators to justice. Though rape still exists in these countries, the topic is discussed more openly and some men have publicly denounced the act as a human rights violation. Men's public acknowledgment of the criminality of rape is helping reduce its shame and stigma and creates more awareness.

Discussing rape and sexual and domestic violence makes the AGILE girls emotional and teary-eyed. During our discussions on the ways women and girls are held back globally, we discussed this topic the longest and many girls shared painful and horrific stories. Like most girls raised in highly patriarchal societies, they've been taught that women are responsible for rape and assault and that they shouldn't bring their abusers to justice, because that brings shame to the victims' families and reduces their likelihood of getting married. Unfortunately, these norms don't help the girls heal from their trauma. I was dismayed to learn from the girls who have been raped that they have become suicidal—some cut themselves and think that they are worthless.

During the discussion, one girl, Anita, started to cry and shake uncontrollably. After regaining her composure, she shared that she was raped twice at the ages of eleven and twelve before she came to the United States. She was first raped as she walked home from school. Community and family members advised her to always walk with friends and to avoid any routes where "bad boys" hung around. After the second rape, everyone, including her friends, insinuated that she encouraged the assaults: "We've never been raped, but you've been raped twice. You aren't the prettiest among us. You must be sending out a signal to entice men." Anita now believes that she subconsciously gives off a signal that makes her a rape target and hates herself because of it. Her mother accuses her of being overly dramatic and states that she, too, was raped as a child yet did not die—she tells Anita to suck it up. Regardless of how much Anita's mother tries to dismiss her pain and family members tell her not to bring shame upon herself and her family by seeking help, Anita is suicidal and desperately wants to deal with her emotions.

Another girl, Kau, shared how angry and bitter she feels and how badly she wants to hurt her rapist. She was brutally raped right here in the Twin Cities by her aunt's best friend's boyfriend. He violently shoved her down the stairs and raped her after she landed on her back. "Don't bother telling anyone because no one will believe you. I'm a respectable man in this community and have a beautiful girlfriend," he said.

Once Kau's aunt got home and found her crying, Kau narrated the painful ordeal and, to her dismay, her aunt reacted as the rapist had predicted. Kau's aunt and friend started to taunt Kau, insinuating that she had a crush on the man and had fantasized about him. After the rape, every time the rapist visited, Kau's aunt would ask her to serve him: "Kau, come and serve food to your husband! He is hungry," she would say while laughing.

A few other girls chimed in that they'd been told the same about an assault they suffered, but that doesn't ease the pain. The majority of the girls have been assaulted within their communities in the Twin Cities, and the community members protected the rapists. It's common within certain communities for adults to know about the perpetrators in their midst, yet the best they do is point out those individuals discreetly to their daughters and say, "You see that man over there? He's a bad man. Stay away from him." Some girls are forced to interact with their attackers at various community gatherings and listen to community members point them out to others, saying, "You see that little girl over there? She was sleeping with Mrs. A's husband. She's a fast little thing." No one questions why a man in his forties would engage in a sexual relationship with a fifteen-year-old girl if he claims it was a relationship. No one calls it by its real name: statutory rape.

The girls then shifted their focus to discuss famous rape cases in the United States, such as at Stanford University and Steubenville High School, where the victims were discredited and blamed for their rapes. The girls wondered how those victims were faring after being violated twice— first by their attackers and then again by being ignored by their communities. The girls wondered if it was possible to have a normal life after a rape. According to the UN, one in three women and one in seventy-one men have experienced physical or sexual violence. In the matter of rape, according to the Rape, Abuse & Incest National Network, one out of every six American woman has been the victim of an attempted or completed rape in her lifetime (14.8 percent completed, 2.8 percent attempted).[18] The girls were extremely surprised to see that the numbers in United States were still that high.

Since the girls wanted to know if a person could have a normal life after rape, I contacted a rape survivor whose work I found online. I hoped that she could provide concrete steps on how to heal from the trauma, deal with the stigma, and continue to thrive.

---

18 "Victims of Sexual Violence: Statistics," Rape, Abuse & Incest National Network (RAINN), accessed April 4, 2017, https://www.rainn.org/statistics/victims-sexual-violence.

JOY MCBRIEN

Joy McBrien is a social justice advocate, dancer, and CEO and founder of Fair Anita, an organization that sells clothing, accessories, and jewelry made from repurposed materials by oppressed and impoverished women, some of whom Joy has worked with in Latin America and Africa.

Joy was raped and traumatized in 2008 while a senior in high school. She suffered in silence, because she feared the stigma that came with being raped and also wondered if others would believe her, especially since the perpetrator was a respectable member of the community. Before the rape, Joy had never experienced or understood oppression. She felt powerless, worthless, as though everything she had worked toward achieving didn't matter; as though her only value to the world was to be a sexual object. It took her two years after the incident to confide in another person about the agony she was dealing with. In 2012, just when she was beginning to see a therapist and start the healing process, she was raped again, this time by two different men on two separate occasions. She was completely mortified—she became more withdrawn and felt completely alone.

Joy was obsessed with how her brain was changing throughout the process and how toxic her thoughts had become. Her fear of going crazy drove her to the internet, where she frantically conducted research on rape. Furthermore, she was consumed with the idea of finding out what violence against women looks like in different cultural contexts; she started traveling outside of the United States to meet and talk with rape survivors. She forged relationships with the women and built connections, which played a critical role in her own healing. "These women are not behaving as victims. They are leaders of their families and communities, and they persevere. They are survivors," she said.

Joy created her organization, Fair Anita, after traveling to nineteen countries and talking with women who have experienced sexual or domestic violence. Initially she intended to start an organization that was focused more on social work, since therapy played a huge role in her development. However, one clear theme arose when talking to the women: the need for economic opportunity. The women, especially those living in some of the poorest communities on earth, needed jobs in order to earn an income. A sustainable income meant the possibility that most of the women could leave an abusive partner, or at least be more valued in their homes, lowering abuse levels. The women would use the money to care for their children. Joy explains this in terms of Maslow's hierarchy of needs: your most basic needs must be fulfilled (food, shelter, safety) before your psychological needs can be addressed. The women she works with are empowered through fair trade jobs. They receive at least three times the minimum wage of their countries, and their advocates ensure that the women are safe and in good working conditions.

As an advocate and rape survivor, Joy knows it is vital for her to work with victims of sexual violence. She is passionate about her work, which contributes to her resilience. She has innate empathy toward the women: "When working with the women, it doesn't feel like I'm coming into their countries as a white privileged woman and trying to save them. It really feels like we're building a community of strong women who have overcome." As an advocate, she reminds the women and their communities that women have the right to feel safe, valued, and respected, regardless of where they live. She teaches the communities about how they thrive when women and girls are fully engaged and included in every facet of the economy.

Joy has helpful tips for other rape victims to survive, heal, and continue to make strides in their lives. Her first and most important piece of advice is for victims to know that the rape or assault they suffered wasn't their fault, regardless of what others say or how much the victim tries to make sense of it. She adds, "I'm aware most victims suffer alone, as they believe no one would believe their story. I want to assure you there are people out there who believe you, believe in you, and want to help. Please do not suffer alone; find someone, anyone to tell. I'm available to talk to. You can reach me at info@fairani-ta.com." She adds that staying in silence and suffering alone fills a person with despair and thoughts of unworthiness. Her second piece of advice is for victims to make time for self-care, which enables them to understand that the negative experience doesn't control their future.

Joy has embraced the art of journaling, which she finds therapeutic. She calls on every victim to find effective and healthy ways to express their feelings if others aren't listening or saying the right things. Besides journaling, she also dances to express her emotions. Joy has been seeing a therapist since 2010, and more recently has enrolled in eye movement desensitization and reprocessing treatment—another form of therapy to desensitize her rape triggers.

As a woman of change, Joy is also involved in several projects to raise awareness about sexual violence and to empower disenfranchised women. In 2009, she worked with a group of local women in Chimbote, Peru, to build the city's first battered women's shelter, where she met Anita, the namesake of

Fair Anita. Joy also speaks publicly about rape and sexual assault. Speaking publicly and being open about her personal experience has helped take away some of the shame, and has helped other women and girls to know that they're not crazy, insignificant, or alone.

Joy believes that it is vital for women to empower one another; we can make a huge impact in the world by the seemingly simple act of loving one another loudly rather than feeding into the culture of women hating on each other. As women of change, we have the power to alter the culture to one where women support each other, build each other up, and invest in each other's successes. It would be a powerful way to change the world—acknowledging and celebrating each other's value.

Joy is always looking to grow her community of women investing in other women. We can support her work by shopping at www.fairanita.com, or by following Joy on social media: Instagram, @fair.anita or @joymcbrien; Facebook, www.facebook.com/shopfairanita; and Twitter, @fair_anita. Joy can also be invited to set up displays of Fair Anita items at house parties and events.

The AGILE girls were curious about how some women find the strength to leave their abusive partners before being permanently disfigured or even killed. A few girls shared that their mothers are battered, yet are reprimanded by community members for not being good wives and for agitating their husbands. Some girls have seen their mothers try to leave, only to be scolded and encouraged by family, friends, and church members to stay and not set a bad example for their daughters. A few girls wondered if it's possible for a woman to live a fulfilling and happy life without a man.

I asked if any of them could stay in an abusive relationship, and a few responded proudly and loudly, "Only if he is fine as heck and everyone knows I'm his girl!" One girl, who was deep in thought, then asked me,

"Ms. LaBelle, what would you do if you were in an abusive relationship?"

"I set boundaries in my relationships and abuse of any kind is something I don't accept or tolerate. I would walk away if those boundaries weren't respected," I responded.

"What if you were in love with him? How do you walk out on a person you love? What if he needed you? My mother says my abusive father needs her and that you don't walk out on someone you love. My friends say the same of their cheating, lying, and abusive boyfriends."

"Girls, all I know is if you don't love yourself, don't expect someone else to. It's about your values and how you want to be treated by others. Remember—you're worthy and valuable. You have to realize you are enough, whole, and complete in your own right, and not look for someone else to make you whole. Before you look for someone to love you, be sure you love yourself first and be comfortable with the idea of being alone as opposed to being with someone who treats you poorly."

After the session, I wanted to reach out to a woman who not only speaks about domestic violence and abuse but is a survivor and gives practical steps about how and why to leave an abusive partner. A fellow speaker and friend at the Minnesota Speaker Academy suggested I contact this amazing lady he follows on social media, Yvonne Sims.

WOMAN OF CHANGE

YVONNE SIMS

Yvonne Sims is an author, speaker, blogger, women's advocate, and a mother to three gorgeous children. She's the oldest of five girls; her father, who was an army drill sergeant, and her mother were strict disciplinarians. Yvonne and her sisters were taught the power of having a great sense of self, discipline, self-sufficiency, and resilience, and the importance of serving others. She's a woman of change who believes in women empowering each other—she shares her life story and lessons learned in order to encourage, motivate, and uplift others. One of her daily goals is to use her life experiences to lovingly remind women that they are powerful beyond measure.

Just six months into her marriage, Yvonne was devastated after getting laid off from a job she loved. Two weeks later, she found out that she was pregnant. What was supposed to be a joyous celebration was met with anxiety. Her husband, Judas, was wealthy and could provide for the family; money was not an issue. However, she loved being self-sufficient and also enjoyed having a job. Additionally, Judas became emotionally and verbally abusive a few months into their marriage. He had never been abusive during their courtship, so Yvonne assumed it was a phase and would pass.

The abuse got worse after Yvonne lost her job and continued throughout her pregnancy. Judas belittled and criticized her daily for not cleaning the house, working out, or getting their business off the ground: "Your days of making good money are over. You will never succeed at anything ever again. You're lazy and have no ambition. You won't make it in this world without me."

She stayed in the marriage, praying that things would get better; she was ashamed to tell anyone about the abuse for fear of being judged and labeled a bad wife. To the outside world they were a perfect couple. Yvonne was considered lucky to be married to a wealthy man. She played the role of the dutiful wife and maintained the image of a perfect, happy home; little did her friends and neighbors know it was all a facade. She continued to make excuses for her husband's poor behavior. Whenever her two older children from a previous marriage asked why their stepfather was always so angry, she defended him: "Judas has a lot on his plate at work. He's working hard to provide a better life for us." Yvonne was also concerned about what their church members would say if she left her husband. As a staunch Christian with tremendous respect for the institution of marriage, she was conflicted—she had already gone through a divorce and was still followed by the stigma.

Regardless of how hard she tried to make the marriage work, things only got worse. Judas eventually physically assaulted her while she was pregnant. For the first time in her life, she contemplated committing suicide, but realized that those dark thoughts were an indication that she needed help. The next day she called her mother and explained everything, to which her mother immediately replied, "How can you give that man so much power and control over your life?" Her mother told her about Daughters of Christ Ministry, Inc., and their focus on biblical counseling. Yvonne started attending weekly counseling sessions, where she learned tools to stand up to Judas. Over time she became more confident and realized that living in an abusive marriage was not God's plan for her life.

Even though she was aware that her marriage was abusive, she found it hard to leave. The push she needed came from her oldest child, when he announced that he was moving in with his father due to his stepfather's abuse. He didn't like the way he was being affected by the abuse and could no longer bear to see his mother being treated so poorly. The thought of permanently losing her son prompted Yvonne to think more of her children's well-being than saving her marriage. It dawned on her then that if her son, who spent half the time with his father and the other half with her, was so severely affected by his stepfather's attitude, her other two children who lived in the house full-time must also be affected. She had to quickly make a decision!

Propelled by love for both her children and herself, Yvonne mustered up the courage to ask a judge for a restraining order. She knew the restraining order was the only way she and the children could safely get out of their home. She had no idea what her life outside of the marriage—the affluent community, fancy mansion on twelve acres of land, and huge parties they threw—would look like. She was certain of one thing: life isn't replaceable, and she and her children would be safe and happy anywhere else. She no longer cared about what her church members would think. She held onto the words of Pastor Marcus Gill: "Do not stay in a bad relationship just to satisfy church members."

Their transition was difficult, which compelled her to share with her followers on Facebook that she and the children had left Judas due to abuse. They only had a few pieces of clothing and were in need of basically everything to start over. The response was overwhelming and the love came pouring in.

Yvonne continued to share her story after settling into

her new home, because she believes it is our responsibility as women of change to share our stories of adversity, challenges, and lessons learned so that other women can avoid similar pitfalls. As women, we are called to be our sister's keepers. Her book, *Trusting I AM: Breaking the Chains of Domestic Violence*, is written in a way that can be used by all women regardless of their marital status. It will help abuse victims get out of their situations and enable others to recognize signs of abuse early on. In the introduction, Yvonne points out the typical characteristics of abusers:

> *Anyone can become a victim of domestic violence. Abusers are cunning, manipulative master deceivers. They come across as kind, generous, helpful and loving. They appear as the knight in shining armor. They woo you with charm, are willing to go above and beyond to help you. They don't wear an "I am an abuser" T-shirt. Instead, they spare no expense into spinning a web of lies, in hope of trapping you.*

> *The red flags tend to be subtle. When you notice kinks in their armor, abusers tend to compensate with praise, gifts or even try to convince you that you are the problem. Don't be deceived. This is a smoke screen. If you are focused on the things they do for you and not why they do them, you miss the key differentiator between a good man and an abuser. Motive is everything. So is pattern. Abusers choose their victim based on their ability to control them.*

Yvonne explains that in order to heal and move on from pain, anger, and betrayal, you have to be resilient and forgiving, not only of others but also of yourself. The key to building up a high resilience is to start small. As you accomplish small goals, stretch yourself and your faith. She likens resilience to running a marathon: if you've never run before, you can't run a mile. Instead, you have to slowly condition your body to walk short and gradually longer distances. Eventually you start jogging, and finally, you work your way up to running, first at a slow pace and then to longer distances at faster speed. There are no shortcuts to resilience. Be patient with yourself. The more you're willing to face and endure, the stronger you become. Another important element to building resilience is to have an accountability partner. She encourages everyone to get a mentor or an accountability partner to encourage them along the path; as she biblically puts it, "Iron sharpens iron."

Yvonne understands that forgiveness is a sign of strength and courage and that it's vital to practice forgiveness in order to move forward. She admits that it isn't easy to forgive when holding onto past hurt, wishing things were different, or staying stagnant due to loneliness. It's important to accept and face reality, and it's OK to cry and mourn the end of a relationship because it brings you to acceptance. However, she cautions every woman not to dwell in crying, which can quickly lead to depression or bitterness, but to mourn and then move on. It becomes easier to forgive when you accept that you're an imperfect human—embrace mistakes as learning opportunities. Yvonne has forgiven Judas for the hurt he inflicted on her and the children, but most importantly she has forgiven herself for putting her children in harm's way and has asked for their forgiveness. She has also forgiven herself for allowing someone else to treat her poorly and for forgetting her worth.

Yvonne provides two important steps for breaking free from any abusive relationship in her book: The first step is to accept the behavior for what it is. She explains that when we care about a person, it's common to make excuses for their abusive behavior. We often see their offenses as isolated incidents caused by some extraneous circumstance; however, when we consistently excuse controlling, demeaning, and harmful behavior, we enable the abuser to continue hurting us. We can't move forward until we accept that there is no justifiable reason for anyone to abuse us.

The second step is to take responsibility for your life. You need to accept that you aren't responsible for your partner's behavior. Your only responsibility is to get help, support, and love in order to get to a safe place, heal, and grow. If you have children, it's also your responsibility to provide a loving, nurturing, and healthy home for them.

After discussing these topics with the girls and interviewing these phenomenal ladies, I realized that the culture of rape and violence toward women is a worldwide problem that needs to be dealt with. This will liberate everyone: the women who are usually the victims and the men who are usually the perpetrators. These issues continue to exist because we propagate a culture that allows and justifies sexual violence against women by accepting misogyny and degrading women for entertainment. There are certain things we can do collectively to end our tolerance for violence against women, to empower both men and women to disrupt the status quo:

- "Call a thing a thing" (Iyanla Vanzant). The rape culture continues despite education about how evil rape truly is. This is a result of violence being accepted as an aspect of masculinity, as well as victim blaming. When rape is addressed from this angle, it is no longer seen as a crime—a violation of human rights—but as an explainable act. Instead of blaming a victim, asking, "Why was she drunk at a party?" we should instead ask, "What made him think it was OK to force himself on a woman against her will?" We should have a zero-tolerance attitude. There should be no excuse for rape or violence and we should call rape by its name.

- Create and teach a curriculum that addresses sexual assault and rape in all schools starting from elementary. In the United States and some European countries, sexual assault curricula exist in schools but aren't taught at every level. However, the students are educated on these topics, which deter certain behaviors. In Cameroon and most of the African continent, Asia, and the Middle East, these topics are missing from the curricula. Young boys and girls are not taught about consent or appropriate and inappropriate touch. If boys are taught at an early age about consent, respecting themselves and others, and how wrong and evil rape, sexual assault, and violence against women are, it will influence the kind of men they grow up to be.

- Teach about masculinity without violence. Once we identify violence in masculinity as the main cause of violence against women, we have to ask: is masculinity inherently violent? How can a man be masculine without being violent? We have to redefine masculinity and teach young boys and men what it means to be a man; to understand that rape or the use of violence against women is not the definition of masculinity. These ideas should be universal and taught in schools, places of worship, businesses, and community events.

- Focus gender studies on the respect for women and emphasize women's rights as human rights.
- Educate communities about the contributions of women in their communities and in history. This could enable even misogynists to see women as full and complete humans.
- Create a safe environment at schools, work, places of worship, and community gatherings for women and girls.
- Allocate money toward the creation of call centers and shelters for victims of rape and violence. The governments in each country, including organizations and businesses, should prioritize this.
- Create sustainable employment opportunities for rape and domestic abuse victims in every community.

TAKEAWAYS

- Stand up and speak out against rape, sexual assault, and violence against women and girls.

- Have conversations with women and girls on the importance of creating boundaries in their relationships, knowing their worth, and loving themselves.

- Develop a high level of resilience and practice forgiveness so as not to buckle under adversity and to continue to make strides in life.

- Seek help to safely get out of a toxic relationship. Life is irreplaceable. If you find yourself in an abusive relationship that looks ideal to the outside world but is a nightmare in reality, choose life.

- Share your life experiences to motivate, encourage, and empower other women. Your story shows others that there is another way and that they too can become overcomers. It also gives them the tools they need to avoid making the same mistakes you made.

DISCUSSION QUESTIONS

- Have you or someone you know been sexually assaulted and felt worthless and suicidal? Reach out to Joy McBrien at joy@fairanita.com, or 1-800-656-HOPE (4673).

- Are you in an abusive relationship? Call loveisrespect's national hotline at 1-866-331-9474 or 1-866-331-8453 (24/7), or the National Domestic Violence Hotline at 1-800-799-7233.

- What can you do to empower and support rape survivors and victims of domestic violence in your community? Share with the group.

- How can you work with others to ensure that there are sustainable employment opportunities within your community for domestic violence and sexual assault victims? Share with the group.

- To grow, we must let go of resentment toward ourselves and to others. Who do you need to forgive? What did you learn from those people who require your forgiveness? What do you need to forgive yourself for? What did you learn about yourself as you forgave yourself? Share with another woman you trust, and ask her to do same. We grow together!

- Build up your resilience so you can withstand adversity and setbacks without crumbling and continue to thrive. Take the following activity to evaluate your resilience level.

Here is a Resiliency Quiz created by Dr. Al Siebert for determining how resilient you are and how you can work to develop better coping skills throughout your life.[19]

Rate yourself honestly from 1 to 5 (1 = strongly disagree, 2 = somewhat disagree, 3 = uncertain, 4 = somewhat agree, 5 = strongly agree). Then add up the numbers of each question and see your assessment below.

Q1: I'm usually optimistic. I see difficulties as temporary and expect to overcome them.

Q2: Feelings of anger, loss, and discouragement don't last long.

Q3: I can tolerate high levels of ambiguity and uncertainty about situations.

Q4: I adapt quickly to new developments. I'm curious. I ask questions.

Q5: I'm playful. I find the humor in rough situations and laugh at myself.

Q6: I learn valuable lessons from my experiences and from the experiences of others.

Q7: I'm good at solving problems. I'm good at making things work well.

---

19 Al Siebert, "Resiliency Quiz—How Resilient Are You?" *Al Siebert Resiliency Center*, accessed September, 20, 2016.

Q8: I'm strong and durable. I hold up well during tough times.

Q9: I've converted misfortune into good luck and found benefits in bad experiences.

Less than 20: Low Resilience: You may have trouble handling pressure or setbacks, and may feel deeply hurt by any criticism. When things don't go well, you may feel helpless and without hope. Consider seeking some professional counsel or support in developing your resilience skills. Connect with others who share your developmental goal.

20–30: Some Resilience: You have some valuable pro-resilience skills, but also plenty of room for improvement. Strive to strengthen the characteristics you already have and to cultivate the characteristics you lack. You may also wish to seek some outside coaching or support.

31–35: Adequate Resilience: You are a self-motivated learner who recovers well from most challenges. Learning more about resilience and consciously building your resilience skills, will empower you to find more joy in life, even in the face of adversity.

36-45: Highly Resilient: You bounce back well from life's setbacks and can thrive even under pressure. You could be of service to others who are trying to cope better with adversity.

Life, as we know, is full of challenges and adversity. The only way to not only survive but thrive is to have an adequate or a high level of resilience. Kendra Cherry wrote a short, brilliant article listing ten steps on how individuals can build up their resilience level:[20]

1. Find a sense of purpose in your life
2. Build positive beliefs in your abilities
3. Develop a strong social network
4. Embrace change
5. Be optimistic
6. Nurture yourself
7. Develop your problem-solving skills
8. Establish goals
9. Take steps to solve problems
10. Keep working on your skills

---

20 Kendra Cherry, "10 Ways to Become More Resilient," *Verywell*, September 18, 2017.

KEY WORDS

Ask for help

Valuable

Self-love

Counseling

Worthiness

Responsibilities

Choose life always

Support system

Acceptance

Sustainable

Shelter

Healthy relationship

Share your story

Resilience

Forgiveness

WOMEN
IN LEADERSHIP

According to UN Women,[21] only 22.8 percent of all national parliamentarians were women as of June 2016. As of October 2017, eleven women are serving as Head of State and twelve are serving as Head of Government. Globally, there are thirty-eight states where women account for less than 10 percent of parliamentarians in single or lower houses as of June 2016, including four chambers with no women at all.

---

21 "Facts and figures: Leadership and political participation," UN Women, accessed May 29, 2017, http://www.unwomen.org/en/ what-we-do/leadership-and-political-participation/facts-and-figures.

CHAPTER SIX

THINK OUTSIDE THE BOX AND DESIGN YOUR OWN PATH

*Big ideas come from forward-thinking people
who challenge the norm, think outside the box,
and invent the world they see inside rather than
submitting to the limitations of current dilemmas.*
—Bishop T.D. Jakes

What is "the box"?

The box, through the lens of patriarchal influence, is the norms, the expectations, and the limitations placed on women. These norms require women to both know how to and love to cook, expect women to get married and have children, and tell women that they can't be breadwinners and can only go into certain career fields. These values are around domesticity, motherhood, and traditional femininity. For example, a woman living in the box is resigned to her role as a homemaker and caretaker. Women may choose this role of their own volition, which of course is a valuable choice for many women and their families. But in too many places in the world, women are forced into these roles without the individual agency to choose for themselves, which discourages them from exploring their own talents, skills, and values that might exist outside the box.

What does it mean to think outside the box?

This means being creative and original instead of following expected ideas—taking a look at yourself and discovering what you value, what is meaningful to you, and what you're passionate about. It means grasping onto your own intuition, agency, and freedom. This can be challenging if you are a victim of the norms, expectations, and limitations placed on you by patriarchal influence. Thinking outside the box means examining the values and talents that drive you and choosing the path that best supports them.

How do you discover what your own skills and talents are? Ask yourself: What am I good at? What do I most enjoy? What did I love when I was a child? What's my driving force? What nudges have I received from the universe about where I should be spending my time and energy?

Thinking, let alone acting, outside the box can be intimidating, especially if you find yourself in a forced role of submissiveness. However, taking that step is not only empowering but liberating, as it forces you to focus on results and not on a prescribed process. It enables you to develop creativity and critical thinking skills.

As women of change, it's imperative for us to think outside the box in order to make an impact, because most females are innately multiskilled and multitalented. A few women uncover their many different talents at a young age, but for the majority, life circumstances eventually force or awaken those hidden talents. However, only those who think beyond prescribed rules and take courageous steps to seize or create opportunities end up living a more fulfilled life. My friend Tambi Makia is a perfect example of how circumstances can compel a woman into uncovering her hidden talents.

When Tambi moved to Bristol, Tennessee, and couldn't find a hair salon where she could get her hair braided, she practiced braiding her own hair. She nurtured this talent over the years and now has the braiding and styling skills of a professional. This is evident in the manner in which she braids and styles her two gorgeous daughters' hair. Like Tambi, some of the women I know have uncovered their hidden talents and are now as skilled as professionals at those talents. Many women realize that they get satisfaction and fulfillment from those skills and want to turn them into money-making ventures rather than hobbies, or would love to devote more time to fully exploiting their skills.

However, due to years of social conditioning and patriarchal influences, women have been taught and encouraged to confine themselves to a template, to only be one thing at a time—a daughter, a wife, and ultimately a mother. This creates doubt and fear in some women's minds, because they wonder if they can handle anything outside the box and if doing so would be the right decision. Some women are lucky to squeeze in other hobbies using skills and talents that are outside the realms of being a daughter, wife, and mother. The rest, unfortunately, still have to find the courage to go after their dreams, especially when their skills are not only taken for granted but referred to as "household chores" or "women's skills."

The lack of support is usually accompanied by discouraging words: "Everyone can do that," or, "Do you really think someone is going to pay you to do that?" These words cause discouragement and create doubts. The biggest roadblock happens when women start to doubt their abilities and let negative words sink in. They eventually become paralyzed with fear and watch their dreams die.

Even though the ladies of this chapter are often reminded that their skills are not up to par with professionals', their talents are still sought after by family and friends. I learned from my grandmother that one way to defeat patriarchal ideas is for women to use their talents to pursue their dreams fearlessly and adamantly.

After Mom retired from her teaching position, she was expected to stay home, raise her children, manage the house, and do nothing else. This was the honorable way for a woman married to a man of Dad's status to act. Dad was fully employed as the Divisional Officer, a position that commanded respect; most referred to him as the "big man." It was considered demeaning for the wife of a big man to earn money or seek any form of employment, especially the kind of business Mom wanted to go into. As a woman of change, Mom didn't buy into society's ideas of what a woman can and cannot do. She loved cooking and baking, so she started selling pastries and other delicious treats. Her pastry business eventually blossomed. This venture was frowned upon by many who considered her ungrateful, disrespectful, and stubborn for earning her own money and not giving her husband the chance to be "the man" and take care of her.

Mom didn't let their negative remarks and rebukes move her from her path. Making and selling treats made her happy and fulfilled and allowed her to earn a living. She was able to maintain her financial independence and was delighted to do what she loved. Her actions set a positive example for her daughters and taught them the importance of not letting anyone else determine their future.

I've realized that using your skills and talents doesn't necessarily mean going to school—it's an alternative path to your dream. It's about seizing the moment and designing your own path. Following your dreams, talents, and passions is not always linear. We become stuck when we believe that there is only one way to approach life or earn an income. To think outside the box, find alternate ways to achieve your dreams and take the necessary steps to bring those dreams to life.

In my work with women and girls, I realized how gender norms and a feeling of incompleteness keep women from achieving their full potential. When MAWA offered grants to low-income women to become Certified Nursing Assistants (CNAs), we candidly interviewed the women and learned that some of them had been dragged to the office by their husbands, who had insisted they become CNAs because the training was free. The husbands, as the heads of the home, made all of the major decisions for their families. Some women shared that their dreams were to become business owners or teachers, yet their husbands objected:

"This is America; you can't become a businesswoman or teacher in this country. You aren't smart enough, you have an accent, and you aren't white. Besides, every woman can become a CNA—it's about taking care of people, something you women are gifted with."

The women didn't want to risk having fights at home, so they relented. One woman added: "What is a woman without a man? I have everything now; I can't jeopardize my marriage for a career."

I was glad to have Mom's experience to share with the AGILE girls, as they are constantly faced with being forced into specific roles; they feel stuck with no alternatives besides doing what society and their parents expect of them. The girls pointed out with despondency that women and girls rarely get to design their paths, because the rules that affect their lives are made by men. They shared their personal experiences with being placed in the box:

A Caucasian girl divulged to the group that her dream is to become an engineer, but her mother wants her to become a nurse or social worker instead. Her mother believes that engineering is a man's field. The girl continues to have fights over her career choice with her mother.

A Somali girl shared that her dream is to become a pilot, but her parents discourage her daily by saying that women shouldn't fly planes. Her parents also remind her that she would be forced to take off her hijab before being able to fly.

A Liberian girl shared that she's gifted with her hands and enjoys cooking, sewing, and braiding hair. Her dream is to become a top chef and introduce Liberian food to the world. However, her parents tell her that cooking is a skill that every woman possesses, and no woman goes to school to learn how to cook. They remark that she should learn something she can't learn at home—something useful.

I shared Mom's story with them as a way to provide inspiration and motivation, and they admired her guts. As I continue working with women, I notice how damaging it is when they think of themselves as incomplete; I've become obsessed with finding out if other women share my sentiments. I wanted to know if these women of change were consciously creating opportunities to reorient and empower women and girls to realize that gender norms are a social construct and nothing more. To give the girls more women to be inspired by, I decided to share stories of other women of change who pursued their passions and flourished in typically male-dominated professions. I came across Kari's story online and reached out to her for an interview.

KARI SEVERSON

Kari Severson is a health and wellness aficionado with the credentials and lifestyle to back up her titles. Born and raised in Minnesota, she considers her childhood to be one of the greatest blessings in her life. She was born to amazing, loving, stable, and supportive parents who instilled confidence and courage and provided their children with go-getter attitudes. She was raised with the "sky's the limit" mentality that enabled her to become hardworking, determined, and daring—to take risks in life, especially business-wise.

Even as a young girl, it was clear to see that she was an entrepreneur in the making. She enjoyed being in charge and taking control of her own affairs. She concocted creative ways to earn extra money rather than waiting on allowances from her parents. She made lemonade stands and would go door to door selling random items from her parents' home. She adds laughingly, "I'm certain my parents wondered from time to time where some of their belongings had gone."

As an undergrad at the University of Minnesota, Kari pursued a degree at the Carlson School of Management, during which she participated in an Entrepreneurship in Action course where she was partnered with a female entrepreneur. Her innovative partner was opening a fitness studio catering to female cancer patients and survivors, called "Survivor's Studio." This initiative had a profound impact on Kari and solidified her interests in entrepreneurship and the health and wellness field. Working with a female entrepreneur who was innovative and determined empowered Kari to focus and break out of prescribed roles. She learned the healthcare side of business by working for UnitedHealth Group and used her two major passions, yoga and running, to learn the fitness side by teaching yoga classes and running marathons.

In the middle of her MBA program, Kari was sedentary for the first time in her life, unable to exercise or stay healthy. When she started taking books to the gym, she knew it was time for a drastic change. She realized she could not make time to exercise because she had so much studying to do. She finally crafted a way to squeeze in some workouts without skipping out on her studies: she would study and work out at the same time! One day while working out and studying as usual, the concept of walking and working hit her like a bolt of lightning. Coincidentally, treadmill desks were just coming onto the scene. She quickly partnered with a top manufacturer to design the Walkway Workstation, which incorporates device charging and internet access into a treadmill desk.

As a woman navigating the world of entrepreneurs and investors (a predominately male field), she has faced her fair share of challenges. She admits that the initial process and concept were intimidating, like going into any new venture is. Male colleagues acted superior to her and attempted to make her doubt her abilities. She was often the only female in the room or the youngest professional at the table. As a woman of change, Kari didn't let fear break down her will but stayed the course, knowing that one way to destroy male superiority is for women to use their talents to infiltrate male-dominated professions. She knew that her continuous success and perseverance would serve as motivation and a driving factor for other young girls who dream of becoming entrepreneurs or inventors.

After gaining more expertise and knowledge, Kari has figured out not only how to survive, but thrive in those environments. Though female entrepreneurs may be few and far between, those rare few have been incredibly supportive of her as mentors, colleagues, and even friends. "If you're a strong and resilient female leader, it actually can be to your benefit to work in a male-dominated environment," she asserts. "It can make you stand out that much more." However, like most women, occasionally she gets questions that reference not only her gender but her role in society: "How do you plan to balance your start-up with raising a family? Do you think it's a good time in life to do something like this, you know, as a woman?"

Regardless of the negative comments, Kari believes that passion is the key to staying the course with any start-up. It's critical to be grounded in deep passion for your idea, or else you will certainly be shaken and eventually give up. She explains, "Passion is the foundation and fuel for your business or ideas; you'll be able to come back to it and tap into it when the going gets tough." From her experience, she knows that it's extremely important when embarking on a business venture to be all-in. To women and girls who dream of pursuing their passions, she repeats the exact advice that her mother gave her: "If you work hard and put your mind to it, the sky's the limit. If you're passionate about doing something, do it!"

Kari hopes that women who have the talents to become inventors and entrepreneurs will do so because of the invaluable contributions they can make to society. She emphasizes that the world is half female and that women are increasingly the majority of graduating college classes.[22] She explains: "We

22 Allie Bidwell, "Women More Likely to Graduate College but Still Earn Less Than Men," *U.S. News*, October 31, 2014.

need these bright young women to apply their unique perspectives and groundbreaking ideas to science, technology, and daily life. If these ideas aren't brought to the surface, we're selling ourselves short as a society."

Kari believes that every human needs to be whole in order to function properly and achieve their goals, and that thinking outside the box helps with this. She equates being whole with a three-legged stool. Your stool sits upon your core foundation, whether that's your faith, your values, your family, or your friends—whatever you hold near and dear to your heart. If your foundation is rocked, nothing else matters, so that's what you must prioritize first and foremost. Then you must address the three legs of your stool. In Kari's case, these are sleep, nutrition, and fitness, and she ensures each leg of her stool is balanced to have optimal performance—to be whole. She calls on the reader to support her mission by developing a healthy lifestyle and avoiding sedentary habits.

Kari feels fulfilled and liberated; she excels in her career because she made the choice to capitalize on what she is good at and passionate about. After learning about Kari's experiences as an entrepreneur and inventor, I decided to share the story of a woman whose journey and success clearly demonstrate the benefits of thinking outside the box. Her journey is one I am familiar with and inspired by, as we are close friends.

WOMAN OF CHANGE

TERESE TANDE

Renowned YouTube and social media chef Terese Tande is my friend and sister. We met in high school at Saker Baptist College and become close friends—we remain very close to this day. Terese was born in Buea in the Southwest Region of Cameroon. Unlike many single kids, she didn't grow up spoiled and sheltered. Her mother taught her the value of hard work, perseverance, self-reliance, and compassion. Her mother's home was always full and bustling with energy from several relatives who lived with them. Terese learned from an early age how to deal with different personality types and co-exist respectfully, skills that are now serving her well.

Terese is a chef, healthy-eating evangelist, fitness enthusiast, television personality, mother, and wife. She holds a bachelor of science in public health with a focus on health promotion and administration. As a chef she has coined the phrase, "Eating healthy doesn't have to be boring." Even as a young child, it was clear to see she had a knack and passion for cooking, so her mother nurtured this passion by giving her new recipes to try. Having a full house also played a pivotal role in developing her cooking skills; there were willing taste-testers available to try out her new recipes. By the age of nine, it was clear that young Terese was a master in the kitchen when she skillfully prepared one of the most difficult and complicated Cameroonian delicacies: *fufu and eru*. This meal has since become her signature dish.

In 2010, Terese was diagnosed with gestational diabetes while pregnant with her second son. The doctors urged her to make drastic changes in her lifestyle. She immediately registered at the gym and started exercising religiously and vigorously. As a health professional, she knew that exercising alone without a radical change in her diet wouldn't help her achieve her desired results. She wanted to continue eating the delicious African foods that she loved, but quickly realized that she needed to make some modifications without losing the flavors and appeal. She began replacing palm oil with alternative and healthier oils, and replacing starchy cassava *fufu* with oat bran *fufu*.

As a woman of change, after noticing positive results she thought of other women who might be going through similar challenges and needed motivation and tips to stay healthy. She remembered the African proverb, "When you educate a man, you educate an individual. When you educate a woman, you educate a nation," and decided to share her journey to inspire others. She also seized the opportunity to fight the notion that cooking is women's work, an injustice that she assumed only happened in Africa but learned existed to a lesser extent in the United States. She was infuriated when she realized the number of men who are top chefs,[23] more than triple the number of women, and the fact that men also earn significantly higher wages. It dawned on her that, when it comes to making money, cooking as a skill isn't looked down upon or considered women's work. She attributes this attitude to the patriarchy—it's a way of men exhibiting superiority over women. "It's like telling women that men are better at everything, even cooking." She decided to become a chef.

With these ideas as the driving factors, she began shar-

---

23 Ryan Sutton, "Women Everywhere in Food Empires But No Head Chefs," *Bloomberg*, March 16, 2014.

ing her food recipes, exercise regimen, and weight journey on Facebook. She hoped that the cooking aspect would inspire other women with similar talents to become chefs. She stayed on course and lost a significant amount of weight within two years, dropping from 214 pounds to 138 pounds. Family, friends, and fans started asking for healthy tips and one-on-one counseling sessions. These requests gave birth to her show, *Cooking with Terese* (CWT).

However, the ideology behind CWT was not embraced by all; some traditionalists accused Terese of modernizing certain African dishes and taking Africa out of them. She responded with logic and explained why she substituted certain ingredients, and most of the critics gained new knowledge. Her personal belief is that cooking is an evolving art, and she continues to spread that message.

Some of her critics have accused her of being too driven for a woman and not spending enough time with her family. She believes it is possible for a woman to have a full-time career and still pursue a passion without neglecting her family. She encourages women to pursue their passion, as it could breathe new life into their souls. Over the years she has developed a high level of resilience, which has served her well. As a woman from a community that honors academic degrees and accolades but snubs creativity and talent, she has gotten negative comments from people who have tried to undermine her passion: "Did you leave Cameroon to become a cook in America?" or, "You must not have a college degree. Cooking is the best you can do; besides, every woman knows how to cook."

Regardless of the naysayers, Terese continues to grow and change lives. Her level of focus, innovative techniques, creativity, curiosity, and boldness to try different recipes are some qualities that differentiate her from other chefs. She encourages young ladies to nurture and develop their passion, even if it's different from their career. Obsessing about developing a talent to make money can easily get in the way of fully exploiting that talent. Instead, her advice is to stay true to your passion and build it up to the best of your ability; the money will come eventually. She adds: "Do what you love because you truly love it. Break the rules, don't do what the world expects of you, but rather be unique."

Terese also advises young women to strive for financial independence and economic success by using their talents. If you can turn your passion into a money-making venture, you can afford a better life for yourself and your children or give back financially to causes that elevate women. She adds, "We live in a world vastly different from that of our grandparents. In this era, a woman's independence is an asset to the entire household—not just a financial asset but also a pivotal lesson to her children, especially her daughters. It informs them that the world is for those who can carve out their own way even in a partnership, without having to depend on another person." She also states, "Women's empowerment is critical to the growth of any society. Women are natural-born leaders, and allowing them to blossom to their full potential benefits everyone in society. Strong women give rise to strong, vibrant, and prosperous societies."

Terese is focused and determined to develop her brand to reach many more people, change lives, and ultimately become a household name. Her cooking show episodes are uploaded on YouTube and are broadcast on the Cameroon Radio Television network and Canal 2 English. This has given her CWT brand significant visibility and growth. Her goal is to ultimately have her passion become her full-time career. As of November 2017, *Cooking with Terese* has 125,655 Facebook followers, making her show one of the most popular African cooking shows in the United States.

Terese has recently incorporated a nonprofit organization, Wholesome Health Promotion, whose mission is to provide nutrition and health education and promote general wellness in rural areas and underprivileged communities in Cameroon. She also plans on using this platform to educate women about how they can use their cooking skills to earn a living and live healthy lives. We can support this initiative by donating to or volunteering with Wholesome Health Promotion, watching her YouTube videos, and visiting her Facebook page.

Every woman needs to become daring and begin to think outside the box. Mom, Kari, and Terese are determined to design their own lives and think outside the box by following their passions. They are living happier lives because of their courage to become their authentic selves and have become inspirations to other women.

TAKEAWAYS

———————————

- Don't design your life to fit into other people's ideas of grandeur.

- Following your dreams and talents is not always a linear path.

- Stick to your guns. When you are passionate about an idea or a dream, don't let others' opinions deter you.

- Develop an active lifestyle. This will keep you more alert, energetic, and healthy.

- When embarking on a new venture, be all-in and passionate. Passion will give you the fuel you need when times get rough.

- Adopt the sky's-the-limit mentality by following Adam Toren's "5 Steps to a Sky's-the-Limit Mindset."[24]

———————————

24 Adam Toren, "5 Steps to a Sky's-the-Limit Mindset." *Entrepreneur*, November 24, 2015.

DISCUSSION QUESTIONS

- What's one move you've made toward following your passion that was unconventional? Share the experience and lessons learned with a friend.

- Write down the skills and talents you've uncovered and brainstorm with the group on how to fully exploit them or turn them into a money-making venture.

- Have you ever gone into a male-dominated profession? What were some of the challenges you faced? How did you thrive? What advice do you have for other women going into typically male-dominated fields? Share with the group.

- How can you implement the skills of a successful entrepreneur, such as passion and being all-in, in other areas of your life? Share with the group.

- What are the components that make up the three legs of your stool? List each on a piece of paper. How do you feed each of those legs appropriately? Share with the group.

KEY WORDS

Multitalented

Investor

Core foundation

Alternative path

Active lifestyle

Maximum performance

Brainstorm

Design

Passion

Liberating

Innovation

Assert

Entrepreneur

Investor

Women's venture

CHAPTER SEVEN

WOMEN HELPING OTHER WOMEN

*True community is based upon equality,
mutuality, and reciprocity. It affirms the richness
of individual diversity as well as the common human
ties that bind us together.*
—Pauli Murray

"Girls compete with each other; women empower one another." As reassuring as this common statement sounds, insinuating that girls automatically empower one another once they become women is false. If girls aren't raised and encouraged to develop self-love, self-respect, and self-worth and to realize that one girl's win is a win for all, with palpable examples around them, they'll grow up to become competitive women. This encouraged female trait doesn't dissipate due to age, because our culture continually tries to create competition among women—not competition with men as other humans, but among other women. Wives and mothers-in-law, women fighting over the same man, "mean girls" gossiping about one another; the examples of women trying to tear each other down in our culture run rampant.

When I was growing up, it was common to see a woman being attacked verbally and even physically at times by her mother-in-law. In certain cases, women were physically thrown out of their homes with few belongings by mothers-in-law for several reasons: not bearing children after a few years into the marriage, giving birth only to female children, or not waiting on a mother-in-law or husband hand and foot. It was considered taboo for a wife to defend herself against an abusive husband or mother-in-law. It was also common to see a woman picking a fight with another woman who was suspected of sleeping with the first woman's husband, or attacking a woman who was seen at a restaurant with the other woman's husband or boyfriend.

But what if we reject this notion? What if we're on each other's side? What if we looked at each other's wins as wins for all of us? After all, when we see a woman rise to power, she's setting an example for other women to follow. All these examples were so prominent in my community that they were normalized.

The Oroko Women's Association tackled each of these problems during their monthly meetings or called for emergency meetings to deal with such situations. If women were fighting with each other over a man, both women were fined for disrespecting themselves. I remember an incident when two women combined forces and beat up a man for carrying on a relationship with both of them. They realized that they had a problem with the philandering man, not each other. On the issue of women fighting with their daughters-in-law, Mom reminded the members that their son's wives were women facing similar challenges and were other people's children. Mom always asked the women to imagine how hurt they would be to learn that their own daughters were being beaten or treated poorly by their mothers-in-law. The association also fined members who fought with one another for any reason, as well as those who spread malicious rumors or gossiped about something a member shared in confidence within the group.

I believe that the reason Mom is the leader of the various groups she's a part of is that she commands the respect of others and many people look up to her. She always leads by example and demonstrates a high level of self-restraint. Mom has a lot of self-respect, possesses high standards, and always stays cool amidst mayhem. One thing she's adamant about is never getting into a fight with another woman, regardless of the situation. Even though her sisters-in-law often come over to the house to pick fights with their brother, Dad, and drag Mom's name into their issues, she never joins in. She goes about her business as though she can't hear what they're saying. If the bickering gets too loud, she steps out of the house. Yet, when the same in-laws are in need, Mom is the first to lend a helping hand. Though she sometimes calls people to order, she doesn't stoop to their level. I admire her calmness and marvel at her willingness to help others, even those who don't get along with her. Mom explains:

"Iya Makane, it's not that I don't feel like retaliating when others are being mean to me. I do. But, you have to be able to tell when someone is trying desperately to get you to do something out of your character and then refuse to give them the satisfaction. Those women are Dad's sisters, and I have to respect their relationship. I won't jump into the middle of their fights even when they drag my name into it. Dad doesn't need me to fight his battles; he can handle the conflict with his sisters. If I get involved, it will become three women fighting. I believe in women helping each other rather than fighting with one another."

Mom is the epitome of class and grace, and she exemplifies what sisterly love and respect for self and others should look like.

When I started reading *Fearless Girls, Wise Women and Beloved Sisters* (which I discussed in chapter 3 of this book), I called my dear friend and sister, Tambi Makia, to discuss the absence of positive, strong women and the frequency of evil stepmothers and wicked mothers-in-law in the stories we were told as children. We examined the effects those stories have had in our lives.

I personally cannot count the number of stories about evil stepmothers and extremely wicked mothers-in-law that I heard as a child. Those stories of wicked mothers-in-law terrified me away from the notion of marrying a man with a living mother. Selfish, I know, but I figured it would be excruciating to live most of my adult life with an evil mother-in-law whose only mission in life would be to make mine miserable. This sentiment was not mine alone; Tambi expressed my exact sentiments. We spoke candidly about how we developed such negative thoughts and feelings toward other women, even though we are women. The answer was simple: they developed from the stories we were told nightly, through the storybooks we read and the folktales we were told around firesides. One of the most common and horrifying stories we were told as kids about evil stepmothers, which I have learned is common in Africa, was of a beautiful young girl named Wase.

When Wase's parents suddenly died, she lived with her vicious stepmother. Her stepmother and her two stepsisters were envious of her beauty and grace and made her life miserable. Wase worked tirelessly all day and night and wasn't allowed to attend school. Her stepmother also made sure she went to bed hungry many nights.

One evening, the stepmother sent Wase with her favorite clay pot to the stream to fetch water. The stream was miles away and it was raining heavily. Once Wase got to the stream and stooped to fill the clay pot with water, the heavy tide swept the pot from her hands. She became frightened and searched for the pot frantically, but it was too dark to see.

Once she got home and recounted her story, her stepmother shoved her out of the hut with instructions to only return after she had retrieved the pot. After searching for hours to no avail, Wase started to cry and sing, calling on her dead parents to send her help. An old woman appeared and asked what the matter was, and Wase explained the situation. The old woman asked Wase to help fill her jar with water, which she gladly did. The old woman then produced a new shiny clay pot to replace the missing pot and also gave her three golden eggs with instructions on how to use them. Wase thanked her profusely, filled the new clay pot with water, and proceeded home.

Once Wase got to the entrance of the village, she struck an egg and a huge mansion appeared. After handing over the water to her stepmother, Wase headed out and struck a second egg at the village square; all sorts of food and delicacies appeared at her mansion. She struck the third egg and many maids and servants appeared.

When the stepmother learned of her fortune, she insisted that Wase share the secret. Wase did but cautioned the stepmother to adhere to all the instructions.

The stepmother sent her daughter to the stream with in-structions to lose the pot on purpose. Wase's stepsister did the complete opposite of everything Wase had done. She refused to help the old woman fill her pot with water when asked and yanked the three golden eggs from the old lady's hand without a word of thanks. Once home, she, her mother, and sister locked themselves in a room and barricaded the door and windows to keep their for-tune from others. She cracked all three eggs at once and spiders, scorpions, snakes, and other venomous creatures filled the room and beat them all to death.

When Tambi and I touched on this topic of evil stepmothers, we realized that a few of our dear friends and sisters are now stepmothers. Our hearts went out to them as we understood that they could be living this perceived nightmare of the evil stepmother, saddled with the daunting task of constantly proving that they mean well. We were amazed to realize how we'd been conditioned from childhood to be terrified and distrustful of other women—to be cynical and judgmental of other females without reason. These stories of wicked mothers-in-law and evil stepmothers also filled our minds with the notion that as women we are inherently bad and evil. What a demeaning and destructive way to have to think of yourself—having the constant reminder that your gender is evil destroys one's sense of self, worth, and value.

The steps taken by the association to create more unity among women in Bekondo yielded positive results: the women un-derstood the power of sisterhood and developed the spirit of networking. One of the reoccurring themes in my conversations with the AGILE girls is competition among women and how it is promoted in many ways, creating chaos and distrust within our gender. The girls believe this is one aspect that makes our gender weak and divided and that, if it were eradicated, we would be stronger. A few girls confessed they are fans of televisions shows such as *Bad Girls Club*, *Real Housewives*, *Love & Hip Hop*, and *Teen Moms*. Though these shows depict women hating each other, fighting over every little thing, using profanity, being overly dramatic, and showing a complete disdain for one another, the girls continue to watch the shows that they defend as depicting the real nature of women as "haters." These shows not only help to normalize women fighting with one another but also portray this fighting as an ingrained trait. This negative and over-the-top attitude makes for good television ratings and glamorizes infighting among women. Many teenage girls look at combativeness and feistiness as attributes to emulate and adopt.

The theme of competition among women is repeated in many children's stories as well, such as tales of romantic rivalries. The usual causes for the rivalries are looks and men, fostering the idea that, as women, we can't trust one another and are envious of each other, especially if the other woman is attractive. This promotes the notion that beauty is something that puts us in danger among other women—that our rivals will go to great lengths to undermine us. In "Cinderella," for example, Cinderella's stepsisters are envious of her beauty and compete against her for the prince's affections by mutilating their feet.

One of the television series that immediately comes to my mind when discussing two women fighting for a man's affection is *The No. 1 Ladies' Detective Agency* starring Jill Scott. In one scene, she's called to the home of an old man with two wives to investigate a frequent case of suspicious food poisoning. At dinner, both ladies are shown fighting with one another over who should feed the old man. The ladies literally try to spoon-feed him as they engage in a spoon fight, pushing and hitting each other's hands. All the while the old man sits with his hands over his mouth like a naughty child who is adamant about not eating.

During one of our discussions on this topic, I asked the girls for ideas and suggestions on ways to deal with this problem. The majority of the girls stated categorically that the problem of competition among women can't be exterminated, because it's common among women across all ages, ethnicities, and races. A few suggested that if women and girls start to uplift one another, advocate for each other just like we do in our group, and make intentional and deliberate acts to stand in the gap for other women, we might create unity.

After this suggestion, I searched online for local women who are already doing this kind of work: creating opportunities and standing in the gap for other women to inspire, uplift, and motivate other women. I know it's not easy to undo centuries of conditioning, but we'll never know how much positive impact we can make if we never try, and the ladies I talked to are giving us ideas on ways we can make positive changes. The key to being the change we as women want to see in the world starts with us fighting against the negative stereotypes we have about our gender and taking actions to empower ourselves and others.

WOMAN OF CHANGE

JEN BISWAS

Jen Biswas is an entrepreneur, mother, wife, runner, coffee drinker, and self-described Jesus follower. She is a Minnesota native with a kind smile, a big heart, and a bigger passion for helping the less fortunate. Jen was raised with her two siblings by two loving and kind parents, whom she credits with instilling within her the love of serving and the true meaning of compassion and empathy. Ever since she was a young woman, she has been active in church and sports.

In college, Jen studied health education with the aim of helping adults live healthier lives. After graduating from college, she worked a few jobs doing exactly what she had intended and thoroughly enjoyed the experience. After working as a health educator for a while, she felt that it wasn't what she was called to do and started searching to find her true calling.

During her soul-searching period, Jen got invited by a friend to go on the World Race. Going on short-term mission trips was something she had always enjoyed in the past. The World Race lasted for a year and allowed Jen to work with various ministries and nonprofit organizations around the world. This extended trip made a huge and significant difference; she got to know clients on a personal level. The organizations Jen partnered with worked with women in difficult situations: women who were sex trafficked or abducted by the Lord's Resistance Army, domestic abuse victims, HIV-positive widows, or girls who grew up as orphans. These organizations provided the women with counseling, education, medical support, and employment so they could fully recover and live hope-filled lives.

As a woman of change, after that year abroad, Jen became relentless and determined to do something to support the organizations and to share their stories with more than just family and friends. She saw the women they had served as her sisters, their problems as hers, and their wins as wins for all. Jen set out on a mission to become an advocate for their causes and to create a store with products that would make a difference in the world—products created and handcrafted by the women themselves. Over the years, she has found organizations that have matched her heart for marginalized women and has curated a collection full of their products called Paisley + Sparrow, with the following mission statement:

> *"To be a marketplace that carries only high-quality, beautiful products where you can be confident that your purchases are making a difference in the world. We want you to be confident that with each purchase you make, you are giving a woman in Ethiopia a way to support her family, a marginalized woman in India a hopeful future, a woman recovering from addiction a second chance, and the opportunity to change a life by your generosity. Thank you for helping us make a difference in the world."*

Jen's project and business empower marginalized women in several other ways. All of the partners she works with are creating sustainable employment as well as educational opportunities for disenfranchised women in their countries. The women are able to feel dignified with jobs and have a way to support themselves and their families. Jen believes it is vital for men as well as women to see how they can take actions to support marginalized women not only in their communities but in other parts of the world, because when women are marginalized the whole community suffers. She asserts that, "We can, and should, support one another!"

Jen spreads her mission using social media, blogging, and word of mouth. As with most start-ups, her biggest challenge has been to drive traffic to her site and make her name known. She adds, "I can't keep going if I don't make sales, so ensuring I sell enough products is my biggest challenge."

Regardless of the challenges she faces, her mission is so powerful and intentional that it gives her strength to keep pushing through, knowing its success will be lifesaving to a group of marginalized women and their children. As a change agent and an entrepreneur, she has learned to deal with speed bumps while always remaining positive and hopeful. Whenever she gets frustrated, she looks back at the past and gets some perspective, realizing just how far she's come. Jen believes that every woman has the right to use her skills and talents to go after and achieve her dreams if the opportunities are available. In cases where women and girls are marginalized and are refused access to opportunities, it's the responsibility of women of change to fill the gap.

We can each support Jen's passion for marginalized women by purchasing items from her store online on Facebook (Paisley + Sparrow) and Instagram (@paisleyandsparrow) or by sharing her page. Jen can also be invited to display her collections at house parties or events.

While putting together stories of women who have made it their life's mission to provide opportunities to enable other women and girls to become the best versions of themselves, I met a gracious lady, Dawn Morningstar, while taking a course at the Minnesota Speaker Academy. I was inspired by the driven force behind her speaking platform. Her zeal and passion to enable women to live an authentic life are infectious and inspiring.

DAWN MORNINGSTAR

Dawn Morningstar is a master certified life coach, speaker, award-winning author, mother, podcast host, and founder of Venerable Women, an organization she began in 2013 to empower and support women to become their authentic selves, live their best lives, and make positive change. She has a glow about her, a magnetic presence that seems to pull people toward her. Her demeanor assures people that they're with a person above pettiness.

Dawn was a pupil at a Catholic school the first time she experienced gender discrimination and male superiority. As a Catholic, her greatest desire was to become a pope or priest. Her dreams and spirit were crushed upon learning that girls were not allowed into the priesthood and that her only option was to become a nun. She was devastated and questioned why girls weren't allowed into the priesthood. The reverend sisters accused her of insubordination and disciplined her for asking too many questions. She stayed quiet on the matter, but deep down she knew it was wrong to keep girls out of the priesthood solely because of their gender.

Her career choice soon shifted when she encountered a successful, charismatic female lawyer her father had hired to represent him in a suit. She was fascinated by the lawyer and remarked to her father in amazement:

"Dad, I didn't know women were allowed to become lawyers!"

"Dawnie, you can become anything you want if you work hard," her father assured her.

That assurance from her father propelled her into thinking of becoming a lawyer, and she realized that women are capable of going into any field they desire.

After recognizing her love for encouraging and uplifting others, Dawn realized that she could instill hope and confidence into others, especially women, who'd been told they couldn't do specific things because of their gender. She began coaching women and men, striving to enable them to live up to their highest potential. After coaching a mixed group for almost twenty years, in 2012 Dawn suddenly felt the need to clearly define whom she was to work with from that point on. As she does when in need of guidance, she reached out to the Divine for inspiration. While meditating, she got the conviction: she would only work with women, and would call them "Venerable Women." As she eloquently puts it, "The words 'venerable women' blew in on a holy wind."

The word "venerable" means "worthy of honor and respect by virtue of our wisdom." She realized that this was the most befitting title and an accurate description of women. She explains that the concept of venerable women is for women who are awakening to their highest selves, women who are on a journey to wholeness and living authentically, and women who are thoughtful and enlightened. Dawn makes it clear that at their core, all people are venerable and worthy of honor, love, and respect--and that women are well-suited to help others remember that about themselves.

In her quest to fully describe a venerable woman, she came up with twelve attributes every woman needs to abide by through asking questions and observations. She named them the V-Attributes and the women later renamed them the V-Attitudes. The 12 V-Attitudes are steps Dawn asserts that, if practiced diligently and consistently by women, will enable them to live their best and most authentic lives.[25] Dawn started to host gatherings with women who were awakening to their best selves and hungry to live up to their full potential to discuss the V-Attitudes. She was pleasantly surprised to see women in their twenties, thirties, and forties among women in their fifties, sixties, and seventies.

Relationship with Self

1. *A venerable woman empowers herself* by using inner awareness to fulfill the needs of her body, mind, spirit, and heart.
2. *A venerable woman embodies her highest and best self* by safeguarding her values, accepting what is, and being authentic.
3. *A venerable woman affirms the depth of her worth* by accessing her finest self, making inspired choices, and doing what is hers to do.
4. *A venerable woman creates and manifests powerfully* by using intention, intuition, and feeling.

Relationship with the Divine

5. *A venerable woman delights in a transcendent relationship with her Divine* by committing to a meaningful spiritual practice, receiving fresh inspiration, and living in sacred union.
6. *A venerable woman calls forth grace in each moment* by being present, embracing peace, and engaging fully in life.
7. *A venerable woman lives as an expression of the Divine*

---

25 Dawn Morningstar, *Venerable Women: Transform Ourselves, Transform the World*, (Venerable Women LLC, 2016), 182–183.

by acknowledging the presence of the Divine within her, knowing her soul, and using her gifts.

8. *A venerable woman expresses joyful abundance* by being grateful and generous and believing in her innate prosperity.

Relationship with Others

9. *A venerable woman uplifts each life she touches* by practicing compassion, unconditional love, and kindheartedness.

10. *A venerable woman loves and is beloved* by inspiring deep connection, trust, and collaboration with others.

11. *A venerable woman embraces the cycle of life* by honoring her ancestors and sharing virtue, wisdom, and traditions across generations.

12. *A venerable woman transforms the world by* transforming herself, contributing to humanity's evolution, and connecting with all that is.

In her attempt to equip more women with the tools to live up to their highest potential, Dawn wrote a book (and audiobook) called *Venerable Women: Transform Ourselves, Transform the World* to explain the twelve V-Attitudes in depth so that every woman could understand and be able to practice them. The book, she asserts, will serve as a specific road map and set of guidelines for women to see themselves as venerable—the main idea from which the twelve V-Attitudes originated. The main question the book strives to answer is, "What is it we as women can and should do to live our best lives, transform ourselves, and transform the world?"

Dawn knows that if the book is written in this manner, answering these questions without being preachy, a woman in

any part of the world who picks up the book will be able to figure out how some of the concepts resonate with her. She says
it will be refreshing to see women of all ages share this kind of
philosophy of empowerment with one another in a nonjudgmental way. Regardless of a woman's age, Dawn believes she
should find out how valuable she is and not base her sense of
self on what society dictates.

As a woman of change, Dawn is aware of the incredible power of being whole, knowing that body, mind, and spirit are one.
When we are whole we are living to our fullest, allowing the Divine to flow through us. The notion that women need to have a
man in order to be whole or complete is incorrect. Being whole
means recognizing that happiness arises within us independent
of external forces. Dawn believes that women are the cake in any
relationship, and that our partner becomes the icing on the cake.

Dawn believes that one way women can reach their highest
potential is to work with and uplift other women. She operates
and believes in the spirit of collaboration, women helping each
other to succeed in our endeavors rather than competing with
each other. Dawn modeled this by sitting down for an interview with me to help me gather enough material for my project while she was in the middle of writing her second book,
Venerable Women: Transform Ourselves, Transform the World.

Dawn is certain that one way to break the practice of competition among ourselves would be for women of all ages to
create gatherings to uplift and empower one another. In doing
so, women would realize that we have similar struggles. Before
starting a gathering of any sort, she advises the leader(s) to
create an atmosphere of confidentiality, safety, and trust, without betrayal. There should be shared leadership, equal time,
and complete attention given to all speakers. There shouldn't
be any form of advice given to any speaker unless they ask for

it. Instead of offering advice, Dawn suggests asking the speaker leading questions such as, "What do you think?" "What do you want to do?" "What outcome do you hope to achieve?" These questions will allow the speaker to look deeper into herself to find answers and solutions, because everyone possesses solutions to the problems they face. Dawn also encourages women to meditate and be in the present. The present moment is the only time when we are at our most powerful and closest to the Divine. When we look back we often become stuck in the past, and when we look into the future we become filled with fear. The present is where great things happen and huge impacts are made.

Dawn believes it's vital for women to develop a high level of resilience and to learn to practice forgiveness in order to thrive through our adversities. Tenacity and resilience are gifts we all possess—gifts we only need to tap into when needed. She describes forgiveness as an important part of personal liberation and believes that we can each reach a place where forgiveness is no longer necessary once we see that every past incident has been for our own growth and evolution. We will still feel pain when someone hurts us, but we can transcend the pain if we look at it as something meant for our growth. This new way of looking at betrayal allows us to have greater compassion for ourselves and others, and will give the capacity for understanding and love. She encourages everyone to come back to love and compassion amidst pain—to always come back to the Divine.

You can support Dawn's work in women's prisons, halfway houses, and shelters by visiting www.VenerableWomen.com.

After reaching out to these women and being inspired by their work, I decided to share the story of a woman whom I've had the pleasure of working with for many years and learned a great deal from: my mother.

MELISSA NAMBANGI

Ms. Melissa Nambangi, or Lady Melisse as she is fondly referred to, is an executive director, journalist, mother, sister, and woman of change. She was born in Cameroon, the first of eight children, to E.B. and Z.M. Nambangi of blessed memory. While working as an advocate at a battered women's shelter, she witnessed significant disparity among African clients. These clients' needs weren't met for several reasons, including language and cultural barriers. The advocates treated them poorly and scolded them: "When in America, speak English!" At other times: "We thought abuse is part of the African culture. Why are you in a shelter?"

Lady Melisse, who is fluent in English and French, became a great asset to the women from French-speaking countries. She soon befriended another advocate, a Liberian native named Ada Beh, who also worked at the shelter. The two women worked after hours to help the shelter's African clients with their resumes, job searches, and other information relevant to new Americans. They soon realized that there were many other African women in the Twin Cities in need of the same services as the shelter clients.

This gave birth to the Minnesota African Women's Association (MAWA) in 2002. Lady Melisse chose the acronym MAWA for a couple of reasons, one of which being that the word MAWA sounds African and means different things in several Bantu languages. Ada stayed with the organization from its inception until 2012.

In 2004, the African Girls' Initiative for Leadership and

Empowerment (AGILE) was created in response to the MAWA women's requests for Lady Melisse to create an empowerment program for their daughters, who were new to the country and felt unwelcome. As a woman of change, Lady Melisse knew the power and importance of empowering young girls and took on the challenge. I instantly became a volunteer with the program.

The AGILE program soon became the most successful and requested program of the organization, and I became the program director in 2007. In 2010, college preparation became the main focus of the program based on the state reports that showed a low rate of African students graduating from high school and enrolling into post-secondary institutions.[26] The organization then introduced an annual three-day overnight college visit during spring break to expose forty girls to colleges outside of the Twin Cities. A health education/teen pregnancy prevention curriculum was soon added as part of the AGILE program based on a high rate of teenage pregnancy.

The organization received a backlash from men and women in certain communities who accused the organization of trying to Americanize their daughters by teaching sex education. They insinuated that teaching youth sex education is like giving girls permission to become sexually active. For this reason, no other African organization addressed the teen pregnancy epidemic that plagued the northwestern Hennepin region. Parents and community members instead proposed that AGILE talk to the girls about decorum and proper etiquette that society deems desirable in good girls: to stop wear-

26 "Minnesota Measures 2007 Report on Higher Education Performance," Minnesota Office of Higher Education, accessed October 20, 2017. http://www.ohe.state.mn.us/pdf/minnesotameasures.pdf.

ing shorts, tank tops, and any revealing piece of clothing that could entice men. They further accused AGILE of filling their daughters' heads with ideas of grandeur by encouraging them to go to college rather than encouraging them to stay at home after school to learn how to cook, keeping in mind that no man would marry a woman whom he considers indecent and who cannot cook.

Lady Melisse stood her ground and through the AGILE program introduced the Becoming a Responsible Teen curriculum on teen pregnancy prevention, HIV/AIDS, sexually transmitted infections, and making responsible choices. We were aware we couldn't achieve our desired results if only girls were taught about teen pregnancy prevention, so the course was taught to both boys and girls. Ultimately, there was a huge drop in the rate of teenage pregnancy within the communities that were plagued the most. There was also an increase in high school graduation rates and college admissions within the communities we serve.

MAWA also adopted a nationally recognized financial literacy curriculum that was taught to the women and girls after we learned that most of the African women had very little financial knowledge and had experienced financial abuse in their relationships. The organization also received funding from the state to provide scholarships to low-income women and girls to be trained as Certified Nursing Assistants (CNAs) or Trained Medication Aides, because the majority had indicated their interest in becoming nurses.

The AGILE program proved what a huge difference it makes when girls are empowered at an early age. When we started the program, about 90 percent of the participants indicated that they would become nurses in the future. They'd been told that it was the best they could do as African girls in the United States. More than 80 percent indicated that they would get a two-year college degree after high school; a four-year degree was just not attainable in their minds. After working with the girls for over ten years, the changes have been phenomenal. The majority of our participants who graduated high school enrolled in four-year colleges and went into diverse fields: medicine, law, engineering, social work, and teaching, to name a few.

The AGILE program has come full circle and the young ladies have become women of change. Some of our participants in college have been hired to work with MAWA over the years; others have become mentors and tutors. From inception until today, the program has served over three thousand girls and seen over one thousand girls enrolled in colleges. The demand for the AGILE program is increasing based on its success, in spite of the lack of funding. The organization continues to seek partnerships, collaborations, and other sources of funding to continue on with the program.

Each of the women mentioned above is taking steps to uplift and empower women and to demonstrate just how powerful our gender can be when we stand in the gap for one another. By creating gatherings where we can uplift and empower one another, we can see our similarities, realize what a powerful force we are when we know our worth, and work together. Creating opportunities for other women enables them to become self-reliant and helps dissipate insecurity and comparison. When women are empowered, it creates a ripple effect. As women of change, we should find ways to create opportunities for other women.

TAKEAWAYS

- Recognize and be empathetic to the plight of disenfranchised and marginalized women; take the necessary steps to elevate and empower them.

- Create opportunities for young girls so they will recognize just how valuable they are and develop a sense of self and a can-do spirit. This way, they won't have to struggle as grown women.

- Choose collaboration over competition or working in isolation. When we work in collaboration, we realize just how much we have in common and how much stronger and more powerful we are when we work together.

- Practice and master the act of being in the present; the present is the only time when we are at our most powerful and can make positive changes.

- Empower disenfranchised women by providing them with sustainable employment so they can become self-reliant and take care of themselves and their families.

DISCUSSION QUESTIONS

- What's one way you can become a woman of change as far as removing competition among women within your community? What steps would you take to achieve that goal? Share with a friend.

- What's one thing you can do to start empowering young girls within or outside of your community? Share with a friend.

- What are some of the things you can do to foster collaboration among women and girls in your community? Share with the group.

- How do you stay in the present? What activities or mind exercises do you perform in order to achieve this goal? Share with the group.

- How can you ensure that the services you provide for others do not become a handicap or an aid, which renders them lazy or makes them dependent on you, but actually empower them to become self-reliant? Share with the group.

- Patriarchal influences tell us that other women are competition, not allies. How do you find yourself competing with other women? Is she your mother? Your sister? Your best friend? Your colleague? Your female in-law? Your enemy? (And if she's your enemy, why?)

KEY WORDS

Courageous

Sustainable

Purpose

Selfless

Collaboration

Powerful

Disenfranchised

Dignified

Venerable

Opportunities

Self-reliance

Authentic

Empathy

Awakening

CONCLUSION

A man who takes away another man's freedom
is a prisoner of hatred, he is locked behind the bars
of prejudice and narrow-mindedness . . .
The oppressed and the oppressor alike are
robbed of their humanity.
—Nelson Mandela

I hope you enjoyed reading *Women Who Soar* as much as I have enjoyed writing it. As I said in the introduction, this book is about challenging us to be women of change by disrupting the status quo—challenging us to become change agents who not only empower and uplift themselves and other women, but also think of how the next generation will be affected by our actions. This book is also a call for men to become men of change—change agents with the foresight to realize that we all suffer and are cheated when women are discriminated against and held back, men who recognize that their voices are powerful and needed in the fight to achieve equality. The shared stories should serve as a motivation and inspiration to all women regardless of their age, race, ethnicity, religion, and culture. They matter; they are valuable and are change agents who can transform their and others' lives.

When asked why people hold onto certain practices, I've been told, "This is the way it's always been done," though this is a cowardly response. We're meant to evolve and grow, not to stay stagnant, holding onto ideas that aren't progressive. There's no better time than now to be conscious of the power and doctrine of egalitarianism—equal rights and human dignity are gaining ground all over the world. More people are beginning to realize that both genders can accomplish a lot more together rather than subscribing to the idea that men are superior and women are inferior. This is the time to challenge gender norms without fear of being accused of disrupting the status quo. My plea to each and every one of you is to start by challenging the gender norms and roles within your homes. The real change of our society begins with us.

I now realize that we are our best selves when we live our most authentic lives. One person getting ahead in life or becoming what they were created to be does not interfere with the journey of another person. We each want to be our best, be happy, have choices, receive grace and compassion, and be free. Let's want the same for others regardless of our differences. We aren't truly happy and free when we oppress others; we're prejudicial prisoners.

We are all born with special talents. It's our responsibility to use our gifts to make the world better and to help others do the same with their unique abilities. Our gifts complement each other and make life easier and better for all.

I've given you a road map and compass with the action items and discussion questions to allow you to look within yourself and awaken to your true self; to provide you with ideas and steps to become a change agent—a woman or man of change. Get into small groups, go through the questions, and start talking about the changes you want to see in the world and how individually and collectively we can make these changes happen—starting with you.

THINGS EVERY GIRL AND WOMAN SHOULD KNOW

- You're a complete and full human being.
- You're worthy of respect and honor.
- You're irreplaceable—unique and special. There is only one you.
- You can't find happiness in someone else; it arises within you independent of external forces.
- You weren't just created for marriage and procreation.
- You're allowed to set boundaries in relationships.
- You're intelligent.
- You have a purpose.
- Your value and worth are not tied to your virginity.
- Marriage is not an achievement.
- Abuse is never your fault; speak up if you're in trouble.
- Not all men are misogynists.

THINGS EVERY GIRL AND WOMAN SHOULD DO

- Have a sister circle.
- Seek knowledge.
- Love books and education—no one can take that from you.
- Be comfortable in your skin; don't be ashamed of your body.
- Strive to be whole; your body, mind, and spirit should be in alignment.
- Be your own competition; always thrive to be a better version of yourself.
- Be smart about money; strive to achieve economic success.
- Be assertive; stand up, speak up. Advocate for yourself and for other women.
- Reject gender roles.
- Reject the culture of women hating on other women.
- Be fearless and courageous.
- Practice being in the present: the present is where great things happen and huge impacts are made.

ACKNOWLEDGMENTS

Writing this book wouldn't have been possible without certain amazing women who have greatly influenced and impacted my life; women who I am privileged and blessed to call my family. Heartfelt thanks to my beloved grandmother ("Mom"), who taught me and all her daughters to have a sense of self-worth, to be self-reliant, and to remember the necessity of being allies of other women. My gratitude goes to my mother, Melissa Nambangi, who taught me about the power of standing in the gap for other women and the importance of creating opportunities to empower disenfranchised women and girls. My gratitude and love to my beloved aunt and second mother Judge Beatrice Nambangi ("Auntie Dawdaw"), the backbone of the Nambangi family, my prayer warrior, and the most selfless person I know. Your unconditional love for me gives me the strength to keep on keeping on. You are the rock upon which I stand. I love you dearly. To my aunties Inez Nambangi-Kalle and Sandra Nambangi-Kruch, thank you. You teach me every day about being resilient and a go-getter. Your unwavering love and support encourage me to become the best version of me. I love you all.

Heartfelt gratitude to my beloved late grandfather, Z.M. Nambangi ("Dad"), who taught me and the rest of his off-spring that we are inherently equals, not just in words but in action. You inculcated in us the love for education and learning. Your actions proved to me that there are good, intelligent, and upright men who love, respect, and honor women.

My love and gratitude to my witty, intelligent, creative, and darling brothers, Cyril ("Dada") and Sidney ("Yummy").

Thank you for the love, encouragement, and support. A deep and profound thank you to my uncles, Victor ("Captain"), Eugene, Paddy, and Rogers, for sending good vibes my way and checking up on me always. Uncle Ro, thank you for always standing in the gap in prayer for me, always believing in my abilities, and never having doubts in what I can accomplish. Your fervent faith in me pushes me to set higher goals for myself.

To my friends and sisters, your love, support, and encouraging words give me the courage to continue making strides in life. Your support was invaluable during this process. I appreciate and cherish each and every one of you. My heartfelt gratitude to Njenja Motuba-Ngwambokong, Joyce Nweteyim, and Henrietta Abuengmo-Nsesih. You ladies have demonstrated to me over the years what sisterhood is and proven that time and distance do not destroy a true friendship. Thanks for being my allies.

A deep and profound thanks to Tee Tande, not only for agreeing to be interviewed for this project but for always stating categorically, "Sis, you've got this. I am here if you need anything." My love and gratitude to Ma Nyen Tambi Makia: your kind words, contagious enthusiasm, and continuous excitement throughout this project—"Belle, I can't wait to make some noise on social media when this book is done. I am proud of you"—gave me strength on trying days. You are awesome and I appreciate you.

My heartfelt gratitude to Divine Arpellet for personifying loyalty, dependability, and love; for sending uplifting devotionals my way; and for assuring me in a way only you can that all the time and finances invested into this project were going to pay off—"Cherie, I am praying for you and I can't wait for the New Year. 2018 is your year of new and exciting things." Cherie, those devotionals were encouraging, especially on challenging days. Thank you. Thank you, Amy Long, for texting me every week, "Sis, how can I pray for you this week?" and for consistently checking up on my progress on this project. A warm and loving thank-you to Nene Etinge for checking up on me regularly and reminding me often of how much you believe in me and are praying for me. You continue to remind me that empowering girls is something you've always envisioned me doing since we were teenagers. Thank you to Lidia Sanguma for the encouraging words and for stating doubtlessly—"Ms. Belle, you are doing what you were created to do." Thank you, Iverte Njume Samme-Ekane, for checking up on me and reminding me you were praying for me, though you had no idea I was working on this project.

My heartfelt gratitude to Reuben George not only for being a man of change and the best kind of friend anyone could ever ask for but also for being so supportive. You ran around this city printing numerous copies of the manuscript when I needed them and letting me bounce ideas off you. Thank you for also speaking prophetically over my project regularly—"Ms. LaBelle, this book will be bigger than you ever dreamt of. Just you wait and see." Thank you for being an honest, thoughtful, considerate, and genuine friend.

Thank you, Valery Nchako, my witty and assuring friend, for stating always, "Iya, you are a smart, intelligent, and driven woman. I know the book will be great."

To the people who contributed greatly and helped to make this project a reality, thank you. My sincere gratitude to Jennifer Ally Kern, who introduced me to Amy Quale of Wise Ink Publishing and gave me useful pointers every first-time author needs. Thank you, Ms. Linda Ruhland of Spirit of Success, for sitting down with me, listening to me talk about my book idea, and giving me suggestions on how to approach this lengthy process. You pointed out that I could write at least five books out of the draft I presented to you. I look forward to taking on that challenge.

Thank you, Marcia Malzhan, not only for agreeing to be interviewed for this project but also for your great insight about book publication. A deep and profound thanks to Dawn Morningstar for being gracious and granting me an interview. Thank you for enabling other women to live up to their full potential. My gratitude to Dr. Verna Price of Girls in Action for all you do to empower young girls to take their rightful place in society. Thank you for being a part of this project. Sincere gratitude to Yvonne Sims; you are truly your sister's keeper. You put me at ease the very first time we spoke—it felt as though we had always known each other. Thank you for sharing the lessons learned from your personal experiences to teach other women about the importance of self-love and resilience and to provide them with tools to get out of abusive relationships.

Profound gratitude to Hilda Bih: you, young lady, are a force of nature. In spite of your physical challenges, you diligently typed out all the responses to the questions I asked you and sent everything to me on time. Thank you to Terese Tande of Cooking with Terese: sis, you are simply awesome. A heartfelt thanks to Joy McBrien of Fair Anita: yours is a labor of love. Dr. Edwige Mubonzi, you are a force to be reckoned with. Thank you for standing up for the disenfranchised women in the Congo and for using your God-given skills and talents to save lives. Asante sana. Thank you to Jen Biswas of Paisley + Sparrow for enabling marginalized women to use their skills and earn an income. My gratitude to Kari Severson of the Walkway Workstation. You have proven that it is paramount for women to think "outside the box" and take risks.

My deep and sincere gratitude to Victor Ibeh, Rob Okun, and Gilbert Salazar: thank you for being men of change and fighting against gender disparity. You are impacting a new generation of men who will stand up for equality, respect, and fairness regardless of gender. Your work is invaluable for the fight to achieve a gender-just world. Thank you all for trusting me with your stories and granting my request for an interview to gather materials for this project. You made this possible.

My deepest gratitude and love to my friend, bestselling author, and Oprah's Book Club choice for summer 2017, Imbolo Mbue. You are a rare gem. You took time off your busy schedule to go through my manuscript and wrote an amazing foreword. After all these years, you have remained humble and gracious. Thank you the brilliant write up. I appreciate you.

My sincere gratitude to the staff and interns of Wise Ink Publishing—Amy Quale, cofounder and CEO, for making this process less stressful and for being a joy to work with. Graham Warnken, my writing coach and editor, for your extraordinary coaching skills and for giving me useful guiding tips. Patrick Maloney, the production manager, for managing and executing this project till the end. Laura Wilkinson, for using your superb editorial skills and transforming this manuscript into a brilliant book. Nupoor Gordon, for your remarkable designing skills and for creating a timeless and aesthetically pleasing book cover. Lindsay Davis, the marketing assistant, for conducting an author's interview with me and marketing me as a new author within the Wise Ink community. Roseanne Cheng, the marketing director, for your brilliant marketing strategies, skills, and expertise.

To my AGILE girls: You challenged me each step of the way and put me to the test often. The challenges, though frustrating at times, helped me grow in more ways than one. They enabled me to become more patient, empathetic, nonjudgmental, and accepting of others' shortcomings. You helped turn our program into a fun, loving sisterhood. You called me out when I didn't live up to the standards I had set for the group and made me a better role model and woman of change. Thank you for trusting me with all your being to lead you in the right direction, to help you when in a jam, to share your deepest and most personal thoughts and experiences. Thank you for becoming young women of change and aspiring to be change agents within your communities. Over the years, you became my daughters, nieces, and little sisters. I am honored and blessed to have known and worked with each and every one of you.

Gratitude to Mercy Fomeche Nkeze and Nancy Ngufor Nkafu. Thanks for being my friends and sisters.

Most importantly, my gratitude and thanks to God Almighty, for making this project possible and for making me cross paths with the right people to work on it.